STEEL CITY PRESS

This first edition published in 2020 by Steel City Press, 9 Ravenscroft Close, Sheffield, S13 8PN.

Rebooting Brexit:
The year that changed politics
ISBN 978-1-913047-13-9

Copyright © 2020 John Tennant

Most photographs:
Copyright © 2020 Avit PR
Reproduced by kind permission

CONTENTS

Foreword - by Nigel Farage   **Page 4**

Introduction   **Page 7**

Chapter 1 - The first battleground   **Page 12**

Chapter 2 - Getting down to business   **Page 28**

Chapter 3 - The Parliamentary maze   **Page 46**

Chapter 4 - Do or die?   **Page 61**

Chapter 5 - The zombie Parliament   **Page 71**

Facts and figures   **Page 90**

Chapter 6 - The calm after the storm   **Page 97**

Chapter 7 - Flag-gate   **Page 102**

Chapter 8 - The Brexit door   **Page 110**

Collage of behind-the-scenes Brexit pictures   **Page 120**

Postscript   **Page 124**

Acknowledgements

With express thanks to my family, friends and colleagues for their support over many years of upheaval. Without your support, I don't think I'd have had the strength to keep going.

FOREWORD
BY NIGEL FARAGE
(Brexit Party Leader)

When I first met John Tennant, he was a slightly awkward young man who now resides in Hartlepool, a post-industrial town which had suffered much from the decline of heavy industry and the depredations of decades of EU inspired policies on a whole range of issues. It had always been a stronghold of Euroscepticism, being one of the very first towns that had returned explicit Brexiteers to the Council and had been an epicenter of the great Leave vote in the referendum of 2016. It had voted 70% to Leave, one of the highest Leave votes in the country. Not for nothing was it to play host to the end of the first leg of the March to Leave we organized in the Spring of 2019. An event set up to highlight the failures of Mrs. May's government to deliver the Brexit that the country had voted for.

Like John, Hartlepool is no fashion plate, but also like him it is representative of hundreds of towns and millions of decent, ordinary voters who put their faith in the democratic institutions of the UK, and who had been badly disappointed by the political elite.

These areas, now called the Red Wall, surprised pundits when they crumbled under the Conservative onslaught in 2019's

December election. But this was no surprise to anyone who had studied the rise of UKIP, Euroscepticism at large, and the resounding success of the Brexit Party.

John arrived in Brussels in 2008 as a junior researcher and immediately proved himself a hard working and diligent aide. I couldn't have imagined then that he would move from being an NCO in the poor bloody infantry of Brexit, over a few short years, to being a European Parliamentarian in a new Party. He rejoined me in 2019, not as a staff member but as part of the phalanx of elected members who changed the world of British politics. My surprise is nothing, as he makes clear in these pages, to his own.

This short book is a personal tale of the work, trials and tribulations of a small group of men and women from all backgrounds who worked and played hard to ensure the freedom of our nation.

It is a heartfelt story of one cog in the engine of democracy over a period of a year. A year of political and constitutional madness. The emotions displayed here run like the rides at South Shields' Ocean Beach. It is a story of hope, optimism, hard work, laughter and betrayal, despair, despond, and rightfully pride.

Never in recent history has so much decency and dishonesty been crammed into such a few months of our political life as a nation. John not only had a ringside seat but was a full participant in much of the floorshow.

It has been a pleasure and honour to work with John, and the other sung and unsung heroes that he mentions. I hope that none of us will have to do this, or anything like it, again.

If you want to experience what it was like to smell the greasepaint of our political circus of the last couple of years, then this short book is an excellent primer.

It reminds us of how touch and go the situation really was at the time. It talks of the proliferation of parties, the legal challenges, the zombie parliament, and the attempted putsch for a second referendum with humour and a lightness of touch. Today it feels that in the end we were always going, to coin a phrase, to get Brexit done. But that is not how it felt at the time, and in these short pages, John reminds us how close the gap is between defeat and victory, and how many compromises, never pleasant, have to be taken to achieve a greater goal.

Nigel Farage, Kent, 23/08/20

Introduction - Why this book?

I begin writing this reflection in my final week as a Member of the European Parliament. Just 45 minutes after Nigel Farage made his final speech as an MEP, 20 years after he was first elected to represent Britain's interests in Brussels, we've just voted on the final Withdrawal Agreement in Brussels.

It's a feeling of jubilation. The moment will forever be etched in my memory; I feel truly privileged not only to be a part of the Brexit movement, but to be present and participate in this historic moment. It's a bittersweet moment: I know full well how bad the Withdrawal Agreement is. I know the difficulties that it will cause us later. It's so bad that we've agonised over how to vote on the final deal, but ultimately we are the Brexit Party and we must back Brexit. If we voted this deal down now, we would never live it down: we'd be seen as the Brexiteers who voted against Brexit. We hold our noses and press the button for Yes.

12 years ago, I began my journey to fight for Britain's independence. Little did I believe at the time that I would be a member of the last group of British MEPs to take up seats in the European Parliament. Yet there I was, both a participant and enjoying a ringside seat to the event which will define our generation: the United Kingdom regaining our freedom and independence from the European Union.

Whilst in my final year at University in 2008, I'd seen Nigel

Farage on Question Time and felt compelled to support the need for Britain's independence. Such was his charisma, and the clarity of his argument, that Nigel was able to attract attention over and above a pretty dreary typical Question Time panel.

I'd always believed in independence. Our politicians may let us down, but they are *our* politicians: if they don't do what we tell them, we boot them out at the next election. We should always be in control of our own affairs, something with which membership of the EU is simply incompatible. I sent off my membership application to UKIP and sent Nigel Farage an email offering any support I could.

UKIP at the time was a tiny party. They were glad of the support, and I was even invited by the Party to apply to become a candidate in the 2009 European Parliament Elections. By the summer of 2008 I was the third MEP candidate on the North East list. At the age of just 21 I was a political novice: passionate, enthusiastic and keen. I began my own political journey. The world of politics, the highs and lows, would turn the next twelve years of my life into a constant rollercoaster ride with so many ups and downs. We all believed in the cause, but at the time Brexit was so far off the political radar that the word Brexit hadn't been invented yet. We could scarcely dare at the time to believe that the primary objective of leaving the EU would be achieved within such a short space of time.

It was a decade of highs and lows. We had the jubilation of a tiny party surging to prominence in 2009, then the sadness of what happened in 2010. There was the surge in popularity from 2012 onwards, winning the 2014 European elections, the excitement of winning the Clacton by-election and the devastation at the later in-fighting. Then came the 2015 General Election: a success by any objective measure, but sadness that we'd not managed to replicate the 20%+ that we'd been polling at the end of the year before. There was the euphoria of sweeping to victory in the EU referendum, then the heartbreak of seeing the party destroy itself in the following 18 months. At its peak, the factional scheming would have put Ancient Rome to shame.

I can't even begin to describe the emotions, the bonds of friendship that were forged during those campaigns. It became a party in search of a cause, desperately scrambling around, turning on itself and then onto religious issues. My decision to leave UKIP in January 2018 after ten years of continued membership hurt me as deeply as any relationship break-up ever could: it was so terribly sad that it was proven necessary. They had sealed their own downfall, which was painful to watch even from afar after I'd resigned.

As time went by, it became more and more clear that Brexit itself was being betrayed. We had a Parliament either unable or unwilling (or more likely, both) to deliver upon the referendum result: with 17.4 million votes, the biggest democratic mandate the British people have ever given for anything in history. With the Conservatives lacking a backbone, and UKIP having abandoned the field, there was now a significant risk that remain-supporting parties could capitalise upon the opportunity before them.

Thinking about those days, I cannot help but reflect upon the many thousands of supporters who have given their time and money to making Brexit a reality, some of whom have long since passed away. Their efforts and the Brexit Party's deserve their place in history. Theirs is a legacy that must be talked about for years to come.

I'm writing this short book in the memory of those hard-working, freedom-loving people who answered the call when it was needed. Their efforts deserved to be chronicled. The Brexit Party's role in stopping a second referendum must be remembered, and – of course – the way that it kept the Tories 'honest', forcing them to remember where at least some of their spine had once been located.

After the referendum result, the first stage of Remainer grief was denial. They couldn't possibly admit that they had lost. We were treated to every accusation under the sun, from claims of overspending (though Remain outspent Leave by 3:2), breaches of electoral law (though repeated court cases found in Brexiteers' favour), and frankly bizarre allegations of Russian interference.

The MP for Broxtowe Anna Soubry strongly believed that there should be a second referendum, a so-called 'people's vote'. Who, we wondered, did she think had voted last time? Remainer after Remainer added more voices to the chorus. There was a real risk that Brexit could be torn apart, with suggestions of pitting 'Remain' against 'Stay in the Customs Union' on a second-referendum ballot paper asking us to choose between Remain and Remain-Lite. Politics had lost touch with reality to the extent that a referendum without a credible Leave option on the ballot paper was being seriously contemplated.

In the face of their growing threat, we needed a response. We needed a new political party. We got the Brexit Party. Perhaps the most successful short-lived Party in British history, few others achieve in many decades what the Brexit Party achieved in its first few months. It was the Brexit Party's job to make sure that the gravy train would come to a long-overdue stop.

There were many twists and turns in my seven months as an MEP, many moments to treasure and moments that I'd rather not go through again. The story must be told. We should not forget. This book is partly a tribute to Brexit, but it's also your behind-the-scenes insight into some of the remarkable events that were going on just outside the public view.

Chapter 1 - The First Battleground

"I haven't spent 25 years of my life to simply roll over and to allow a career political class to betray that result" - Nigel Farage

A year before that historic vote in the European Parliament, we had a different Prime Minister. We had a hung Parliament, a Remain-heavy lobby, and we were staring down the barrel of a second referendum. They were uncertain times and a strong response was needed to protect the people's democratic choice made at the 2016 referendum.

Nigel Farage launched the Brexit Party alongside Leave Means Leave Chairman Richard Tice on April 12th 2019 at the Coventry BG Penny factory, where he announced the first of many new European election candidates. We learned the first of a drip-feed of surprises: Annunziata, the sister of arch-Tory Jacob Rees Mogg, and successful businessman Benyamin Habib. They were ready to give up their anonymity, and throw their weight behind making Brexit happen.

Annunziata's announcement as a candidate was a coup. It sent a very strong message that we were serious: we had credibility and quality in both our message and our candidates. Ben Habib told me that he had reached the end of his tether with Theresa May and that he had expressed his lack of faith in the Government to his work colleagues. He explained that he'd had every faith in Theresa May when she was saying all the right things – then spoke of the profound disappointment which came with the realisation that she had no intention of delivering a genuine Brexit.

Ben was no particular fan of Mr. Farage. When he was asked if he'd like to speak with Nigel, he hesitated – concerned about Nigel's supposedly uncompromising and borderline-controversial views. Their productive meeting changed all that:

not only did Ben's original prejudices towards Nigel evaporate, but he asked Nigel what he could do to turn things around. Nigel sensed a man of real calibre, and floated the idea of candidacy for the London electoral region. The rest, as they say, is history. A highly-experienced and well-informed candidate joined the Brexit Party team. A strong, new political vehicle was gradually being built to force the Government to listen to the electorate.

The Brexit Party's roots can be traced back to Richard Tice's Leave Means Leave organisation. It was set up almost immediately after the 2016 referendum: Richard attests that he felt there was sufficient evidence, even in those early days, that there were too many voices of opposition determined to torpedo the referendum result. He thought that threat must be met head on - and neutralised. Leave Means Leave offered Theresa May the benefit of the doubt in her early premiership: she had made all of the right noises. Her Florence speech went down well with many Brexiteers and it seemed, for a time, that Brexit would be implemented on time.

Then came the infamous Chequers summit of July 2018. It wasn't even a deal. It was a UK negotiating position, yet it felt like a surrender document. Privately, even some senior Tories who had supported Remain were expressing disquiet. If that was our negotiating position, what on earth would it look like by the time the European Union had watered it down? Boris Johnson resigned. David Davis resigned. Steve Baker resigned. The wheels were already beginning to fall off. Brexiteers were losing confidence in her ability to lead the nation on Brexit. Nigel Farage was invited to join the Leave Means Leave platform to fight for a real Brexit.

Leave Means Leave were determined to keep up the pressure. They organised a well-publicised march from Sunderland (chosen for its symbolism as the first city to vote to leave in 2016), timed to arrive in London on March 29th 2019. The day that we should have left the European Union.

For some months prior to the march, there were murmurings and discussions. Was a new political party needed to create an electoral threat? Polling commissioned in late 2018 suggested that whilst there was some evidence of hostility towards the government, it had not yet reached the tipping-point where people would switch their votes in large numbers. Parliament repeatedly failed to honour the decision to Leave in February and March, with some accepting the 'worst deal in history' – the appalling Withdrawal Agreement which Theresa May had concluded, and others trying to sabotage Brexit altogether.

That tipping point had finally been reached. In the background, the Brexit Party had been quietly registered with the Electoral Commission and planning was well underway to launch the Party ready for its forthcoming European Election campaign.

Its simple, popular slogan was 'Change Politics For Good'. The original plan, 'Fighting Back', was ditched because it seemed too combative. This must, Nigel and Richard felt, be a positive campaign designed to appeal to the whole 52% - not just to a small section of the electorate. The plan was to champion the benefits of independence and avoid the controversial topics which UKIP had embraced.

It had been a shock to many when Nigel announced his departure from UKIP in December 2018 in reaction to the Party's lurch to a more extreme position on religious issues. The appointment of Stephen Yaxley-Lennon (AKA Tommy Robinson) to advise the then UKIP Leader, Gerard Batten, had been the final straw. Nathan Gill and Jonathan Bullock joined the exodus. Both would become valued Brexit Party colleagues in Brussels after the election.

Nigel signs the forms to register the Brexit Party

The Brexit Party had made clear from the very beginning that candidates and the Party's message must be positive, vibrant and focusing on the benefits that Brexit can bring to Britain. There would be no room for extremism, as demonstrated by a breadth and depth of candidates from across the political spectrum. Brexit is not a refuge of the Right: it transcends traditional Left-Right politics. I remember saying to one of my council colleagues that no party in history could ever have managed to get both Ann Widdecombe and Claire Fox, darlings of Right and Left alike, to agree to stand on the same ticket. They were sceptical. It would never work! They'd fall out in the first week! Yet nothing could be further from the truth. Strangely, I witnessed those two political heavyweights agree on far more issues than they ever disagreed upon. It was fascinating to watch.

Louis Stedman-Bryce, the lead candidate for Scotland, is a very sociable person and unashamedly out and proud. His opening line *"I stand before you as a gay black man"* got a few laughs, because it destroyed the identity politics of many in the Remain movement, and it really punched home the fundamental message that Brexiteers come from all walks of life.

How could media commentators, itching to paint the new Brexit Party as a bunch of right-wing fanatics, do so when the Party was packed with ethnic minority candidates including a gay black man, and Claire Fox? They eventually settled for attacking her as being too left-wing. Some sections of the press would criticise for the sake of it.

We had candidates from the left, right and centre ground; young and old; male and female – experienced politicians and first-time candidates. Tory MP Lucy Allan even tweeted that the Brexit Party had selected "excellent candidates".

Getting people involved in the organisation and planning of the Brexit Party wasn't always easy. Richard Tice said to me that some had felt nervous about it. One of the things people don't appreciate is just how difficult it is to go out on a limb with no guarantee of a successful outcome. For some it could be career suicide, for others loss of friendships. It really was a time to either go for it or not. There were no grey areas at all: Brexit was being betrayed.

The website was launched, and I'm told over 70,000 people registered their interest - myself included. A supporter subscription of £25 was then introduced and 'membership' grew to around 100,000 over the course of the following few months. Richard has often described it as being like turning on a tap. The Party was up and running, the logo was designed and ready for the ballot papers, and staff were working all hours to administer the Party before selecting candidates for the European campaign.

Over the course of the month leading up to the close of nominations, the candidate announcements came quick and fast. They were an eclectic mix. Martin Daubney, the former editor of lads-mag 'Loaded', joined the former Revolutionary Communist Party member and political commentator Claire Fox, as did the former Chairman of Southampton FC, Rupert Lowe. When it was finally announced that Ann Widdecombe had left the Conservatives and intended to run as a Brexit Party candidate, the news stole a significant march on the campaign. Her endorsement and fighting spirit added a new gravitas to the Party. Of course Ann divides opinion, just like many of the others do, but that's precisely what you get when you have a balance of people from all backgrounds. The media just focuses on some things more than others. The real division was simpler: you were either for or against Brexit; there was no room for grey areas here. You want to know why the Conservative Party got just 8.8%, its worst national election result in history? Because it tried to be a grey area: it appealed to nobody because it tried and failed to appeal to everybody, saying nothing of any note.

These announcements helped to build a strong momentum behind the Brexit Party campaign. Almost 100,000 supporters attended packed-out rallies across the country. I had sent in my application to stand based on the principle that I could not sit by and allow Brexit to be overturned. I sat and watched this phenomenon unfold, not knowing whether my name would be called.

Some days later, I was in the middle of having lunch when I received a phone call from Richard Tice. I was being interviewed, and it was the worst possible time. Richard asked some tough questions on policy, background and why I wanted to stand. We said goodbye after about half an hour, and I returned to my now decidedly cold lunch having no idea if I had done enough to be selected. It would not be until I had collected the nomination forms at the Party offices in London to hand in to the Returning Officer at Sunderland City Council, that I found myself on the North East list alongside the experienced former Conservative MSP Brian Monteith and the passionate Richard Monaghan. I felt honoured to be selected and also quickly felt the pressure that standing in such a crucial campaign would bring. The following morning, I handed in the nomination forms and it was official. Now to get on with the campaign!

I watched the Change UK rally where former Newsnight presenter Gavin Esler and Boris Johnson's sister Rachel were announced as candidates. They say that imitation is the sincerest form of flattery, and Change UK were clearly copying our strategy. There was just one problem: they didn't, in fact, offer change.

The Brexit Party offered change…a grassroots movement being born in an instant. Change UK offered more of the same, politicians expecting voters to fall into line.

Secretly I was pleased when they tried (and failed) to imitate us. It legitimised our strategy – other parties were playing catch-up with us.

I wonder, maybe it seems strange now for me to be talking about Change UK. After all – who were they? They were here and gone in an instant. Just remember that at the time, the Change UK bandwagon was being touted as the new 'Centre' Party. They did receive a fair amount of media coverage and that was starting to show in opinion polls. Today's polls are tomorrow's chip paper if you don't consolidate your gains, and theirs was a party run by amateurs. Professional politicians are not always professional campaign managers. In fact, they're used to having a campaign manager to keep them on the straight and narrow. They had created a vacuum, and political vacuums always lead to one thing: in-fighting. That's probably the only thing that Change UK and UKIP ever had in common. The more polished and experienced Liberal Democrats would eventually hoover up the Remain vote.

Brian Monteith often came to stay at my home in Hartlepool to campaign across the region. This proved very helpful to me as a non-driver, and Brian was always enjoyable company. We travelled to set up campaign stalls in Newcastle, South Shields, Darlington, Middlesbrough, Stockton, Sunderland and Durham, whilst many hundreds of supporters were actively campaigning in their own areas. I received hundreds of emails asking for campaign material: posters, leaflets, garden signs and just about anything else you can think of. People were in and out of my house collecting campaign items and literature. We were taking the North East by storm.

During the campaign I recruited colleagues old and new to head up the campaign in various parts of the region. They came from various different backgrounds: independent, former Tories, former UKIP. The Brexit Party offered a fresh and renewed energy that showed little sign of stopping. Bringing these people onto the campaign made it much easier to get our important message of positivity out there to the public: Parliament may have failed to represent us, but there was fresh hope in the Brexit Party that we could deliver a strong 'Non' to the EU bureaucrats on May 23rd. Without the support of Steve Aynsley, Dot Lynch, Alexis Fernandes, Allyn Roberts, Jo Strachan, Claire Powell and Peter Harris, I don't think we would have had even the most basic of infrastructure to run a region-wide campaign.

In the North East, there has always been a quiet opposition

to the EU, resentful of the lack of support from Westminster and 'London-centric' parties. Throughout the campaign I met a lot of very disappointed traditional Labour voters who viewed their Party as actively opposing their own supporters. This went beyond the Brexit issue. They saw the then leader, Jeremy Corbyn, as someone they could not trust to deliver for the North. I saw the first stirrings of what would become the crumbling of Labour's so-called 'red wall' at the end of the year. Many of those people told me that they would never return to Labour. Remember, the 2019 European Election was a very emotionally charged campaign. Swept up in that current, I truly believed that they would abandon Labour for the Brexit Party in a General Election as well. Hubris? Perhaps. Or maybe our threat to the Conservatives caused them to switch tack, forcing them to (at least temporarily) seal the deal with those voters.

Much of the media privately wish that Remain had won the referendum, so it came as no surprise to me when the attempts to derail our campaign began. I and many of my fellow candidates suffered vicious personal attacks: ad-hominem mud-slinging that had nothing to do with the public interest, and everything to do with character assassination – planning to attempt to destroy the movement itself by proxy. I don't need to go over the specifics. If the scandal is 'aspiring politician told a joke to his friends 10 years ago', it really isn't a scandal worthy of more than a single sentence comment. Still, I want to give a personal thanks to the many people who wrote to me offering their support - including those who opposed my position on Brexit. My faith in humanity was reaffirmed: not everyone falls for the kind of muck-raking that much of the media loves to engage in. For all the unfair efforts to damage our reputations, the public had just had enough of it. They responded to our positive campaign with their votes, giving us an unprecedented number of seats for any British Party in European Election history.

We set the date of Saturday May 11th for a North East rally at Rainton Meadows in Houghton-le-Spring, just at the time when postal votes would be landing on doormats. The day would include an open-top bus tour of Sunderland, Hartlepool and Durham. Nigel Farage turned up as boisterous and entertaining as ever and we set off along with Richard Tice. I had first met Richard in Wetherspoons, Hartlepool after the 'March for Leave' from Sunderland to Hartlepool a few months previously. He came across as a very calm and quiet person, a far cry from Nigel, but he also carried that same determination. Everywhere we went, cars were honking their horns and hundreds of people showed their support. There was a palpable feeling in the air that something truly magical was happening. I remember feeling that it was a bit too good to be true - something was bound to go wrong, surely?

In every campaign, there comes a moment which will forever define the campaign – the moment where, deep down inside, you just know what the outcome will be. I felt it in 2016 when running for Council, and I felt it again in 2019. That evening, the venue in Houghton-le-Spring was packed: standing room only. Seeing that atmosphere, something clicked. That's the moment at which I knew what was coming. It's a feeling that's difficult to express with words: it makes you feel like you're a part of something far bigger than any individual. I didn't particularly care any more whether I was going to win my own seat or not. I just wanted the public to send a big message to those who were working hard to stop Brexit, to demand that never again should politicians ignore the biggest mandate the people have ever given to our Parliament. Polls indicated that the Brexit Party was polling in a 25-27% range. The meteoric rise from nothing to such heady levels showed a level of anger directed at Parliament's behaviour over Brexit.

You've heard of the phrase 'they go low, we go high' – meaning that you shouldn't respond to negative campaigning with negativity, but rise above it. A refusal to take off the gloves, so to speak, can be dangerous. In this campaign, though, as we soared 'high' in the polls, our opponents chose to go 'low' in response. Under threat of libel action, the SNP MEP Allyn Smith had to apologise for suggesting the Party was funded by money-laundering. The former Labour Prime Minister Gordon Brown even contacted the Electoral Commission to ask them to investigate the Brexit Party on the back of a Radio 4 interview between Nick Robinson and Richard Tice, where Robinson alleged that foreign money was coming into the Party. The Electoral Commission immediately put the Party on 24 hours' notice, before turning up at the offices to investigate.

By some incredible coincidence, the media were all right there when the Electoral Commission turned up to make it a photo opportunity for the campaign. Of course, every single allegation turned out to be absolute nonsense – but it's always difficult to prove with 100% certainty that you're innocent of anything, especially when you're not getting a fair hearing in the media.

The Brexit Party agreed to tighten the way that it reported the collection of supporter subscriptions to dot even more 'i's and cross some extra 't's. Allyn Smith settled the case by making a donation to charity after receiving a well-publicised letter from Tice's lawyers.

Suddenly, all these allegations stopped. Five days before polling day. When many postal votes had already been returned. I doubt they did any serious damage. Sometimes, a media fit-up job is so obvious that it becomes counter-productive.

Nigel Farage stood alongside fellow candidates in London and announced to a packed house that the Brexit Party had a "clean bill of health". The attempts to smear the Party had failed. It continued its rise in the polls.

May 23rd, polling day. A momentous day in our nation's history. On a more mundane note, it was also the day that my boiler was due for its annual service. We'd fought a strong campaign and the message was clear, but there was an agonising three-day wait before the votes would be counted. The reason for the wait? It's a bit quaint actually. Different countries vote on Thursday, Friday, Saturday or Sunday. We vote on the Thursday. The European Union's rules didn't allow results to be announced until every other European country's polls had closed. They clearly thought that people in Greece might change their votes based upon the results in Gateshead.

My phone did not stop ringing. Texts were coming in thick and fast, just seconds from the announcement that both Brian and I had won our seats with 40% of the vote. Remember, the North East is the ultimate Labour stronghold. Nobody beats Labour across the whole region. We didn't just beat them. Our vote was more than double Labour's. In fact, Labour only just barely scraped the third seat out of three, pipping the Liberal Democrats at the post in a tight result. Usually the principal opposition party picks up support when the government of the day is unpopular. To say that Theresa May's party was unpopular would be an understatement, yet Labour couldn't take advantage: their confused Remain-ish message was enough for them to lose seats around the country, falling to just ten seats.

My parents were there to support me. I celebrated the victory with them, and my Remain-backing brother even rang to congratulate me. Fellow Councillors Shane Moore (who had just become Leader of Hartlepool Borough Council, and who would later become the first Brexit Party leader of a Council) and Tom Cassidy were there to celebrate with me. The result in the North East was staggering. No party had ever gained more than double the vote of the Party in second place and to pick up the first two seats in a three-seat region. This set a trend for the rest of the evening as the Brexit Party took the most seats of any UK party to the European Parliament in European Election history. I became acutely aware that not only was the night a disaster for Labour and Remain, but also that I was going to Brussels with colleagues, many of whom I had never met. A bit like my first day at school!

The wheels were already in motion before the results had come in. The Conservatives braced themselves for the battering of their lives, and Theresa May had resigned as Prime Minister. The European Elections were over and the momentum was fully behind the Brexit Party. These were heady days indeed. 29 Brexit Party MEPs were off to Brussels and Strasbourg - and no-one (including us) quite knew how well we were going to work with each other.

Ann Widdecombe joins Nigel as she launches her candidacy

Chapter 2 - Getting down to business

"It is, and will always remain, a matter of deep regret to me that I have not been able to deliver Brexit. It will be for my successor to seek a way forward that honours the result of the referendum"

-

Theresa May on her resignation from No. 10

We had won. We allowed ourselves a chance to celebrate for a little while. Many of our candidates, whether they had won their seats or not, gathered at a London pub to regale each other with tales of the campaign. Some were only meeting each other for the first time. I took the opportunity to thank Nigel for having the unique honour of working alongside him as an MEP.

I remember his famous speech to Van Rompuy in February 2010 when he accused the new President of the European Council of having the charisma of a 'damp rag' and the appearance of a 'low-grade bank clerk'.

As a junior researcher at the time out in Brussels and Strasbourg, I'd been sitting in the back of the European Parliament chamber. It was almost empty, as usual, as Nigel spoke forcefully and powerfully. There was a sense of witnessing history first-hand: it would be the speech that defined the beginning of Nigel's crowd-pulling speeches, attracting hundreds of thousands of views on social media. The tone of the speech was the point: calling out the indefensible in the strongest possible terms. When someone rises to become one of the European Union's many Presidents (the EU is brimming with Presidents: the President of the Council of Europe, the President of the Council of the European Union, the President of the European Parliament, the President of the European Commission, the President of the European Central Bank, the President of the Court of Justice, the President of the General Court and the President of the European Court of Auditors – did I miss any?), they should expect to be challenged on their appointment.

Tony Benn's famous five questions for those in power were

"What power have you got? Where did you get it from? In whose interest do you exercise it? To whom are you accountable? How can we get rid of you?". When the previously-unknown Herman Van Rompuy popped up, Nigel's bluntness reminded everybody that our new President's mandate was really no mandate at all. The public had neither chosen him nor could get rid of him.

The phones never stopped ringing. Literally hundreds of media outlets across the world wanted to cover the story. Nigel knew at this point he had broken the media silence on reporting from the European Parliament by making the dreary process much more newsworthy. The Van Rompuy speech - controversial to some, celebrated by others - brought Brexit into the mainstream consciousness over the next decade. Another President, the President of the European Parliament, asked Nigel to apologise. It was a gift. Nigel offered a profuse and sincere apology... to bank clerks the world over. He became a household name overnight.

Enough reminiscing: the 2019 European elections may have been won, but there was work to be done. A by-election had been called in Peterborough after the sitting Labour MP had been found guilty of perverting the course of justice (and eventually jailed). Most jailed MPs step down; Onasanya continued from her prison cell. Between her release and the recall petition succeeding she returned to the Commons, presumably whilst electronically tagged, to vote on Brexit. Yvette Cooper's anti-No Deal Brexit Bill passed a key stage by 313 votes to 312. Onasanya's vote had made the difference. Any chance of securing concessions from the EU in negotiations was gone.

The Peterborough by-election would be an acrimonious fight. The Remain lobby had failed to agree on a single candidate, rumoured to have been the arch-Remainer Femi Oluwole, and only Change UK stepped down.

Our candidate was first-class local businessman Mike Greene, who worked extremely hard and should have been the first Brexit Party MP on the green benches. I went to Peterborough to help with the campaign. In all my years in politics at all levels, never had I seen so many hundreds of people gather to help in an election campaign. The momentum was truly in our favour and that campaign gave the first hints that success might be possible in a first-past-the-post election.

First-Past-The-Post is a difficult system for any new party, fighting against the experienced machinery of the establishment duopoly. Yet by the final week leading to polling day, bookmakers had the Brexit Party as the favourites. It is fair to say that despite starting with no data and no local infrastructure, we did extremely well. We came within 600 votes of taking the seat and causing a real shock to the establishment. The Conservatives had split the pro-Brexit vote, allowing Labour to take the seat by a whisker. Such is the difficulty of first past the post elections. The winner doesn't necessarily reflect the public's opinion - there is a strong case for a more proportional voting system to fairly distribute seats to respect the range of views within society. Nevertheless, we had once again beaten the governing party following our phenomenal success in the

European Elections.

It was clear there was an appetite for a fresh, new Party that offered more than just the typical establishment fayre. The Brexit Party really encapsulated that feeling with a positive outlook for a Britain free of the European Union. We sensed that if Boris Johnson won the Tory Leadership there would be a general election, but the question was when? Would it be before the end of the Autumn, before Christmas or even in the new year? Either way, we had to start getting candidates ready across the country.

Strasbourg is a truly stunning city. It has rich history, architecture and great cuisine. The Parliament, sadly, has none of those traits. It is a poorly-designed building with no real connection to the land it is built upon. Not that this particularly mattered to anyone, because it is also a place where egos can be swept up and embraced with a lifestyle that many would envy. It is also one of the three places of EU institutions along with Brussels and Luxembourg. On my first day as a new MEP, I was taken aback by how much MEPs are viewed with a sense of reverence by ushers and Parliamentary functionaries. "All part of the plan", I remember Nigel once quipped years ago. He was right.

I was given the keys to my office, which had been deliberately situated about a half-mile walk from the Parliamentary Chamber. It's just one of the many little 'digs' aimed at eurosceptics which happen on a daily basis out there. On the surface everything is polite, cordial, friendly and welcoming. Behind the scenes, Parliamentary officials try to make life as difficult as possible for anyone who isn't pro-EU. So, once I had navigated the maze of corridors and found my out-of-sight, out-of-mind office, I discovered a 'welcome' pack containing chocolate, champagne and other gifts from the City of Strasbourg - not the Parliament.

Nigel Farage fielding the cameras as we take up our seats in Strasbourg

It would be very easy for any hedonistic person (particularly if you were a europhile and not subjected to the little tactics that we faced every day) to fall in love with the lifestyle and the sense of entitlement that can easily develop. I resolved that day never to allow myself to be swept away with it all. I was there to get my P45, by delivering Brexit. Of course, Brexit had already been delayed until October 31st – otherwise I wouldn't have been there at all.

One of our internal debates was whether to join a European Parliament Grouping. The European Parliament organises itself through pan-European political groups, designed to force national political parties to work with each other in order to gain speaking time, influence and control over the Parliamentary agenda. This, in turn, is supposed to push MEPs ever further towards a pro-EU stance. But what about joining a genuinely eurosceptic group?

Two of the biggest groups had suffered significant losses: the socialist group (S&D) and European People's Party (EPP) had lost a combined 76 seats. This had shifted the balance of power to the smaller Green Group who had made some gains. There was also widespread reporting that some of the more eurosceptic parties had made gains in Italy and France and formed the largest share of seats in the new Identity and Democracy group.

When you join a group, you take on the 'baggage' of that group. We were, as the largest national party in the European Parliament, well-placed to form a group of our own – except for one minor, inconvenient fact. We were due to leave in four months' time. Which party in any other country would join a group, knowing that it was due to collapse imminently?

Knowing that simple arithmetic prevented us from forming our own new group, we wanted to avoid an unnecessary media frenzy. Could we join the Conservatives and Reformists? That group contains the British Conservative Party. Would it advance the cause to join the same group as the French National Rally (formerly the Front National)? No. It would have been a significant distraction – we'd have spent weeks fending off accusations of being far-right by association. Could we join the hard-left group which includes a few eurosceptics? No. We weren't about to sit in the same group as Sinn Fein.

All the groups have undesirables: the European Parliament was an odd mix of former communists, former fascists, a former terrorist (on the Left), and much more besides. If you think extremism exists in British politics, just wait till you see European politics.

No. We couldn't join anyone else's group, and we couldn't form our own. Too risky. Also, it would distract from our main cause back in the UK. We resolved to be identified as non-attached ('non-inscrit') MEPs.

My first speaking slot was 1 minute (they cut your microphone off if you go over) on the Finnish Presidency of the European Council in the second Strasbourg of July. The topic isn't actually as dry as it sounds: they discuss all the EU's priorities for the next six months. Brexit, of course, loomed large. It was a nerve-wracking experience.

I had to leave the Whip's voting meeting to go to the chamber, navigating the rabbit warren of the main atrium towards the 'death star' - as Martin Daubney once described the Parliament chamber.

I kept checking my preparation notes. The Strasbourg chamber is a huge room and incredibly brightly lit. You are welcomed by ushers as you pass the sign-in board and head to your designated seat. All around me were empty seats (as is often the case) and I sat alone, going through the speech in my head as the speaking time on the big screen to my left came closer and closer. To my amazement all my new colleagues came in, one by one, to sit with me and give moral support. That helped give me more confidence and while I may not have delivered my best speech (I tripped over my first line), my new colleagues gave me the lift I needed.

The President of the Parliament had cut off my microphone before I'd finished! Stumble over a word, and your minute's gone before you know it. Let's just say that the European Parliament is not exactly suited to full debate. But then, most of their ideas wouldn't stand up to detailed scrutiny.

Richard Tice asked me whether I wanted to make an official complaint to the Parliament. A eurosceptic 1-minute speech lasts 60 seconds and no more. When a europhile speaks, their microphone is ruthlessly cut off once they reach 75 seconds after the gavel has been banged several times. It's just another example of the petty lack of neutrality. Some vice-Presidents (think: Deputy Speakers in the House of Commons) tried to be fair and impartial, and I respected them for it. Most didn't. Complaining is never worth the effort. We have to accept it and move on: our job was to highlight the nature of the Parliament and why we should leave the place at the earliest opportunity. Perhaps I should thank the President for cutting me off because it showed the public how we were treated in comparison with their friends and EU fanatics.

Sitting with each other and giving each other support in the chamber when it was one of our colleagues' speaking time was never planned, nor policy. We just wanted to support each other and it became part of our monthly Strasbourg life. It was organic and gave us a real sense of camaraderie. It felt like I was amongst friends, not mere colleagues.

The first time I took my seat in Strasbourg that July, I was personally taken aback by the Liberal Democrat MEPs walking into the chamber wearing offensive T-shirts with the words "bollocks to Brexit" emblazoned across the front and back. This was a political move that badly backfired: the British public are not impressed when they see politicians indulging in offensive language. They thought they were being 'funny' or even 'on trend', appealing to their supposed student base of anti-Brexiteers. It was also, of course, against the rules. Those rules, however, would only be applied if eurosceptics had done it.

When North West MEP Chris Davies uttered the same words in a speech, he merely showed people that he had nothing intelligent to add to the debate. If you must resort to insults to 'win' an argument, you're not winning it at all.

Suffice to say their political stunt failed to have the desired effect and in fact it was the Brexit Party's statement in response to the EU anthem that took the headlines that day. As the EU's anthem (the Ode to Joy) was played, we remained seated. We were in a Parliament which the British people had voted to take us out of. The President of the Parliament deliberately provoked us. He compelled us to stand: *"You stand* for the anthem of another country". But the EU is not a country. It might wish to be, but it is not. He demanded that we show respect not just for the European Union, but for euro-federalism itself. No, we couldn't do that. We stood, and turned our backs. The mainstream media reported that we had turned our backs, but naturally failed to report the context.

Hundreds of supporters applauded us. We had made an immediate impact on our first day. I felt it was a dignified protest and we had made our point and a clear statement that Britain no longer wanted to be a star on somebody else's flag.

You'd think that was enough drama that took place that week, far from it. Ann Widdecombe is small in stature but huge in personality and conviction. Very few people in politics become household names and never truly step into the background, but Ann is certainly one of those people. She commands a huge amount of support and opposition in almost equal measure. She is not one for small talk. I first met her at the aforementioned Durham Rally during the election campaign. Whilst she might be quiet privately, she has an innate ability to excite and cajole audiences - characteristics normally attributed to Nigel Farage himself.

Not one of us knew what she was about to say. Well, it certainly made an impact to say the least. "There is a pattern consistent throughout history of oppressed people turning on the oppressors - slaves against their owners, the peasantry against the feudal barons, colonies...against their empires, and that is why Britain is leaving."

Cue bloody murder from the media. How dare she compare the EU to slavery! Of course, that's the 'game' that the media play. Ann's actual words spoke of 'oppressor' and 'opressed', giving three examples: empire and colony, owner and slave, baron and peasant. The media cherry-pick the one, miss the point, and pillory you every bit as much as that baron might have wanted some upstart peasant to be pilloried in the stocks. Her point was that all oppression should be fought: slavery is, indeed, the archetypal example of oppression. It's a perfectly reasonable point to make, but I'm sure that Ann also knew what she was doing: it takes real bravery to make such a powerful point, knowing how it will be twisted against you - and Ann was the person to do it. For someone who shuns social media, she achieved the kind of trending on Twitter many would envy.

There was a surprise in store for Alex Phillips and Henrik Overgaard-Nielsen. Both were brand-new MEPs like myself. They were chosen at random to be tellers for the election of the new President and Vice-Presidents of the European Parliament. Alex rose up as her name was called, avoiding confusion with the Green Party MEP also known as Alex Phillips (screenplay writers would be able to come up with some great slapstick comedy about that – one Brexit and one anti-Brexit MEP, both with the same name...hilarity could easily ensue). Alex, wearing a bright yellow dress, proceeded to wave the Union Flag in a moment of excitement. That was where her excitement began and ended. It was a long, drawn out count of over 700 MEPs voting on a long list of candidates from across the political spectrum. 14 vice-Presidents are elected through several rounds of voting to join one President. Thankfully, in this case only three rounds were necessary. Of course, Alex and Henrik were prevented from being able to participate with their new colleagues in the Brexit Party for a significant amount of time. The irony was not lost on colleagues that two Brexit Party MEPs had been selected to oversee the election of the Presidents of the Parliament. It is not a job many MEPs would want regardless of political beliefs, and I was secretly pleased I hadn't been chosen myself.

It was the end of the first week. I allowed myself a couple of small beers at the bar before heading to Strasbourg station, and the beginning of the first of many long journeys home. I felt privileged to be among talented colleagues, many of whom would make their mark as time went by.

July had two Strasbourg meetings tabled in just three weeks. The next Strasbourg session was due to hold an election to choose the President of the European Commission. I say 'election', but I'm using the word very loosely. MEPs are given a choice of…one candidate. It's a secret ballot. Nobody can be held accountable for how they voted. Ursula Von Der Leyen was the Commission proposal for its President, which cued a string of Google searches by journalists to find out exactly who she was.

She had the charisma of a damp…no, wait, that was Herman Van Rompuy.

Von der Leyen was the former German Defence Minister and had been the longest-serving Minister during Angela Merkel's successive terms as German Chancellor. It was a classic euro-fudge. Von der Leyen was nobody's first choice for Commission President. The EPP group proposed Manfred Weber; the S&D group wanted Frans Timmermans. However, the recent European elections had led to a severe weakening of the EPP voting bloc in the 'cordon sanitaire'. The 'cordon sanitaire' is a construct that enables the larger groups to negotiate powerful Parliamentary positions and to prevent the more Eurosceptic groups from gaining any influence. It is a stitch-up that proves the EU has no real intention of being a politically balanced body. The balance of power effectively lay with the Green and Liberal groupings, who would naturally prefer a more left-leaning candidate. The right-leaning groups refused to support Timmermans; the left-leaning groups couldn't countenance Weber.

Naturally the Parliament shares various positions between the different groups and through this it became more difficult for Timmermans to get the Presidency and by the same token, the socialist groups would not support Weber. The usual compromise is to give the second-biggest group the choice of President of the European Parliament, whilst the biggest group has dibs on the more important President of the Commission. If this sounds like grubby backroom deals deciding the future of an entire continent, well that's exactly what it is.

The Socialist Group got their choice of President of the Parliament in David Maria Sassoli. Now for the compromise. Enter Ursula von der Leyen. The attempt to offend as few people as possible. Even despite the 'cordon sanitaire' stitch up, the vote was closer than most had expected: von der Leyen received just 383 votes in favour, with 327 against.

Then came her acceptance speech.

"I stand ready for further extension of the withdrawal date should more time be required" – Ursula Von der Leyen

We reacted with some righteous indignation to those words. Delay upon delay upon delay. More than three years had passed since the referendum. We were still not out of the European Union. Already, the President-elect of the Commission was suggesting kicking the can even further down the road.

It was business as usual. The EU was being as obstructive as possible to the possibility of us leaving legally on October 31st. Her words were clapped by hundreds of MEPs across the chamber who did not respect the wish of British voters to leave the EU. Worse, they were clapped by British MEPs – including those from the Labour Party, which had taken an absolute hammering at the elections for ignoring their own heartlands.

July was also the month that the Tory leadership election was beginning to take shape. The two front-runners were Boris Johnson and Jeremy Hunt, and both would go on to the head-to-head as many had speculated. The effect of the unprecedented number of seats the Brexit Party had won on May 26th was clearly playing its part in the Conservative leadership election. The pressure was on to win back the public trust in delivering Brexit - and to do so on time. Parliament did not possess the numbers to pass any withdrawal agreement regardless of who was the leader of the Conservative Party. Everybody knew it. The question on everyone's tongue was when, not if, a General

Election would take place. We had to be prepared. The Brexit Party began a process of selecting candidates from across the country to keep the pressure on and help to deliver Brexit.

What we were about to see was a real battle of wills to see how Brexit could be delivered and move forward as a nation.

"Deliver Brexit, unite the country and defeat Jeremy Corbyn" – Boris Johnson after winning the leadership election.

By this point, Boris Johnson knew he had nailed his colours to the mast. Rarely does a politician risk so much that the wheels may come off. He may have seen off the soft-Brexiteer Jeremy Hunt comfortably, but his main concern lay in the shape of Nigel Farage.

Nigel is a very intelligent politician and tactician. He is one of the few people who can galvanise an argument and make it popular. He is Mr. Brexit. Without Nigel Farage, there would have been no referendum. He became the driving force behind the campaign to leave the European Union in the early '90s, before it was on anyone's radar. He was its talisman, its poster boy, its inspiration.

His number one skill is his ability to make even the most complicated of arguments seem remarkably simple. A polished media performer and public speaker, Nigel attracted both fans and enemies alike. He was now the only remaining figure standing in the way of Boris Johnson's success or failure as leader of the Conservative Party. The theatre in Parliament, like the theatre in the European Parliament, was largely irrelevant except for how it impacted on public perception. The logjam was never going to be unblocked in advance of a General Election. For all the posturing and grandstanding, this would be settled in the community centres, churches and school halls around the country which served as polling stations – not on the green benches of Westminster. Westminster was stale. It was sterile. It was deadlocked.

The argument at the time was not so much making Brexit happen, as making sure that Brexit was actually Brexit. Nigel and Richard (Tice) had set up the Brexit Party to not only ensure the second referendum was taken off the table, but also to ensure that any deal would allow us to regain our ability to govern ourselves. The backstop, Single Market, Customs Union and ECJ were not acceptable to any of us because they aren't compatible with being an independent, self-governing nation. Brexit meant leaving those rules and being able to create our own. Theresa May's deal wasn't Brexit. The public made their voice clear on that in the European and local elections, so Boris knew he had to deliver something different.

In the meantime, the uncertainty from the business community was clear for all to see. A continuous stream of delays or even a second referendum would not deliver the kind of commitments that business needed to trade effectively. This was often misrepresented by political commentators as the 'disaster' of Brexit. Brexit was not the disaster. The constant, nagging uncertainty was. Even as I write these words, deep into a Covid lockdown and months after Brexit happened at least in name, we still await certainty on what our future relationship with the EU will be.

Put simply, business needed a clear direction of travel so they could remodel their operations to suit the market. The battle of ideas was on. Johnson needed to get a new deal and he needed it quickly, or the Conservatives would likely be finished as a political force. That was the stark reality for the Conservatives. There was much speculation as to whether Johnson would get a new deal in such a short space of time, and if he did, whether it would truly qualify as Brexit.

In the Parliament chamber

From back row left: Christina Jordan, James Glancy, Matthew Patten, Claire Fox, Jake Pugh, Henrik Overgaard-Nielsen, David Bull, Nathan Gill, Brian Monteith, John Tennant, Robert Rowland, Belinda de Lucy, James Freeman-Wells, Alexandra Phillips, Richard Tice, Jonathan Bullock, Ben Habib, Martin Daubney, June Mummery, Nigel Farage, Ann Widdecombe, Michael Heaver.

Chapter 3 - The Parliamentary Maze

"We have made a generous offer to the PM, that if you stand for a clean break Brexit, we will stand down and not fight with your candidates" - Richard Tice

Boris Johnson became Prime Minister in late July, to nobody's real surprise. In politics, you learn quickly that nothing very important happens in August. Parliament is closed, and political journalists head off on holiday as much as the politicians. August 2019 was Boris Johnson's honeymoon period, as far as that could go with a divided party and a divided country. There was rumour and speculation, and we had to work to be prepared in case of a snap election, but the big picture didn't change very much.

By the time September came along, we were not seeing any real movement on Brexit. What could we do? We had to keep the pressure on, we had to prepare for a General Election, we had to be on the ball with any announcements from the Commission or the Government. We knew talks were taking place, we knew Labour still backed a second referendum and Jo Swinson had doubled down to reversing Brexit altogether, but what were Johnson and Cummings planning?

That was the problem with not yet having Westminster representation. We had contacts, but we weren't able to influence the Parliamentary arithmetic. Instead, we had to build on the wave of popularity of the Brexit Party. By growing our electoral threat, the Government could not ignore us. They knew as well as we did that an election was on the cards, one way or another, over the coming months.

Behind the scenes, a massive operation was being planned. A European election is top-down. Seats are won or lost in the national media more than local infrastructure. For a new party, the challenge of a General Election is immense. We were rising to the challenge: no sooner had the European elections finished, than we began interviewing potential General Election candidates. Having candidates selected was the number one way of proving our electoral threat. Hundreds of people had applied, so we began the sifting process - analysing their applications before inviting to interview. The quality of some blew me away: airline pilots, successful entrepreneurs, community champions, charity workers – these were just some examples of the kind of breadth of applicants we interviewed. Many were ex-Labour who had lost faith in their former party.

We were not prepared to sit by and allow another Brexit fudge to take place. So began a series of public meetings across the country, where thousands of people came along to show their belief in Brexit. It was a commitment to an independent United Kingdom, a commitment to respecting democracy. Rallies in Colchester, Lincoln, Doncaster, Sedgefield and many more drew crowds in areas of traditional Labour support. This was the platform upon which we would make the case for a Brexit without the backstop, the European Court of Justice, the Customs Union and Single Market.

Remember that at the time, all of those were realistic threats. A Remain-heavy Westminster Parliament was holding a reluctant government to ransom. Relying upon DUP support, Boris Johnson had only a wafer-thin command of the House of Commons – always knowing that some of his own backbenchers would oppose him at all costs.

We took our argument to the working-class towns, talking with people who had voted for our independence and giving them hope that someone was fighting on their behalf. At the Sedgefield rally, I spoke alongside fellow MEP Brian Monteith. We met many of those who attended, and were taken aback by the scale of the anger towards the political establishment. Both Labour and Conservatives had promised at the previous election to deliver Brexit.

We were able to persuade many of my colleagues on Hartlepool Council to join the Brexit Party in order to maximise the pressure on the Government. The Sedgefield rally was a turning point: that was the moment at which many decided to take the plunge. I had worked with many of them since 2016 when I had won my seat to the Council, building a strong opposition. The cracks in Labour's red wall had already appeared in Hartlepool: we had gained minority control of the Council in 2019 with support from the Conservatives – a shock to the Labour Party, which had controlled the Council for as long as anyone could remember.

In those circumstances, as we were working together to improve Hartlepool, their decision to join the Brexit Party was a courageous one. A coalition, yes, but a Brexit Party-led Council really upped the ante as far as our Council colleagues were concerned. The local Labour Party kicked off on social media, but many people were supportive of our move. Hartlepool had voted overwhelmingly (almost 70%) to leave the European Union – the Labour Party apparatchiks failed to comprehend that the people of Hartlepool had meant what they said.

From September 2nd to October 14th, this series of a dozen rallies was a huge success, building upon the success of the

49

exciting, big-statement rallies we'd held during the European campaign. I watched my colleague Robert Rowland speak at the Maidstone meeting following another stormer by Ann Widdecombe, where he uttered the words "we are now in a full-blown constitutional crisis and we must do everything within our power to save Brexit".

Nigel Farage gearing up to speak to supporters at a rally

Meanwhile, the media commentary was about whether Boris could get a deal. They questioned whether he would dare go for a no-deal Brexit, and whether Parliament might oust him, install a caretaker Prime Minister and use a so-called 'government of national unity' to force a second referendum. If it sounds ridiculous and far-fetched now, it was a real risk at the time. One key sticking-point was Jeremy Corbyn: the Labour Left insisted that he would have to be in charge; other parties could not countenance such a possibility given Labour's track record on anti-Semitism.

These were very uncertain times and the anger among Brexiteers was palpable. It soon became clear that Johnson's decision to prorogue Parliament on August 28th (which came into effect on September 10th and was originally due to last until October 14th) was one that deeply divided Parliament and began another legal challenge against the Government.

I was surprised that this move was attempted. I had not expected Johnson to request a long prorogation. Parliament would normally be prorogued prior to a new Queen's Speech. It would also normally be prorogued for the Conference season. Combining both, and adding a fifth week, was pushing it a bit to say the least. The move caused upheaval and cries of a 'dictatorial' decision.

The stage was set for another court case. The Scottish Court of Session and the High Court ruled in opposite directions to each other, and the case was referred to the Supreme Court for a final decision. Many of my friends, family and colleagues asked me at this time whether I thought that prorogation was the right decision. I was torn. To support Johnson's decision would be to legitimise prorogation as a tactic to evade democratic accountability in the future. To oppose it would risk ideological purity trumping pragmatism: Remainers were trying hard to prevent prorogation because they wanted to use the Parliamentary time to undermine and subvert the democratic will of the people.

In effect, Johnson had only added an extra week of prorogation – though it would have also prevented known Remain attempts to curtail the Party Conference season. There were still 17 days between October 14th and 31st for Parliament to debate any withdrawal agreement. If no substantive changes were made, then Parliament had already debated the same issue on the floor of the Commons.

However, a prorogation also meant that the previous Parliament had ended. Some prorogation was clearly necessary: this would be the longest prorogation since that of the Long Parliament of the 1600s, some 317 days to be exact. A defeated Bill could not be brought back in the same Parliamentary session, meaning that prorogation was needed before it could happen.

There was also a strategic case for suggesting that such a long prorogation was a bad idea: it would unite the opposition to Brexit, and result in deeper divisions in Parliament. The chances of a temporary 'caretaker' pro-EU government being installed without public consent had just increased. A quandary indeed. The Supreme Court eventually ruled the prorogation to have been illegal, demonstrating a level of judicial activism which set a worrying precedent.

Meanwhile, MEP colleague Rupert Lowe had had a meeting with Michel Barnier – the EU's chief negotiator. Nigel Farage had many things to say about Mr Barnier in the past, and this time it was Rupert's turn to find out. Barnier's mind is sharp, and he carries himself with an air of importance.

Rupert said that Theresa May's Withdrawal Agreement, which had failed three times in Westminster, was a document so one-sided that such an agreement would only ever be signed by a country defeated in war. Rupert was (and still is) of the belief that there is no link between trade and sovereignty: there is no need ultimately to punish anyone for exercising self-determination. Many of us were of the view that Barnier is an entirely capable individual, but flawed in his obsession with the Single Market. It was flawed because Barnier's strict determination to keep Britain in the Single market was actually increasing support for the Brexit Party. His intransigence was putting such pressure on the Conservative government that it actually weakened the possibility of the EU getting concessions in a new withdrawal agreement.

The deal failed to meet any reasonable definition of the Brexit people voted for: a huge divorce bill, the EU defence policy, EU control over fisheries, 'close regulatory alignment' leaving us effectively subject to EU laws, and UK courts overriden by the European Court of Justice. We would have regained only partial control over immigration.

With impressive pace, a Withdrawal Bill was tabled by the Labour MP Hilary Benn before prorogation came into effect. The 'European Union (Withdrawal) (No. 2) Act 2019' was passed on September 4th following Oliver Letwin's successful motion to allow the House to undertake proceedings on the second reading the previous day. It rather cut the legs off the argument that the prorogation would have run down the clock and prevented Parliamentary Scrutiny. If Parliament could legislate at the drop of a hat before prorogation, then why could it not also do so after prorogation had ended?

The Government was no longer in any form of effective control of the House. Boris Johnson withdrew the whip from 21 Conservative rebels who supported Letwin's motion. The Benn Act, as it became more widely known, legally forced the Prime Minister to request a three-month extension if a deal had not been ratified by October 31st. By taking a no-deal scenario off the table, albeit temporarily, the government's negotiating position was undermined.

The legal default position within the Treaties is that a country which has triggered Article 50 leaves the European Union without a deal, unless an agreement has been reached by that date.

The irony! This Act will forever bear the name of Hilary Benn, the son of the late Tony Benn – who had been one of the stalwarts of the Labour Left for decades. Tony Benn was an outspoken Brexiteer, as many traditional left-wingers are, yet his son oversaw the passage of one the worst Acts ever to come out of our Parliament. It tied the Government's hands and surrendered the one significant negotiating position we had left.

It was on September 24th that the Supreme Court ruled that a prorogation would be unlawful:

"if it has the effect of frustrating or preventing, without reasonable justification, the ability of Parliament to carry out its constitutional functions as a legislature."

They further added that the Government had failed to provide a justification for the decision, its length or the effect on Parliament's ability to scrutinise the Withdrawal Agreement. The forcefulness of the ruling took many people aback: the Supreme Court did not just rule that the prorogation should not have happened, nor direct Parliament that it must return at some point, but it ruled that Parliament had not been prorogued at all. It must continue sitting as part of the previous session, until prorogued again – lawfully, this time.

Crucially, Boris Johnson could not now bring back Theresa May's withdrawal agreement for a further vote. It also meant that Johnson was getting closer to the October 31st deadline. He was left with just two options: to get a new deal in record time, or seek a humiliating extension of Article 50.

Prorogation had turned out badly for the government. It was a poor political move which united the opposition into a frenzy, and damaged the government's own credibility. The clamours began for Johnson's resignation, and a motion of no confidence was mooted. Nigel Farage led the charge, arguing that Boris should offer his resignation to the house to face down his detractors and pre-empt a confidence motion. The behaviour and sheer anger from both sides of the Commons following the controversy was something I had never seen nor hope to see in our Parliament ever again. It was becoming abundantly clear that it was now a zombie Parliament, unable to agree on anything. Her Majesty's Government had now lost seven successive votes with a Prime Minister who was more than forty votes short of a Parliamentary majority. Under any other circumstances, Parliament would have been dissolved for a General Election – yet, in another bizarre twist of fate, the Fixed-Term Parliaments Act meant that Parliament had to vote for its own dissolution. It refused to do so.

Boris Johnson kept attempting to convince voters he would achieve his 'do or die' pledge to leave the European Union on October 31st, notwithstanding the ugly shadow of the Benn Act. Geoffrey Cox, who was then Attorney General, delivered a withering put-down of the state of Parliament in his 'zombie' speech. With echoes of Oliver Cromwell's famous speech to the Rump Parliament, it went viral.

From the sidelines in Brussels, I could see a Remain alliance beginning to take shape. The SNP, Liberal Democrats, Change UK and some Labour MPs were actively calling for an electoral pact. I could see the Brussels mindset, up close and personal. It was strange for me: I saw the other side's reaction in more detail than I saw our own. They scented blood. They hoped everything was now so chaotic that with a few more turns of the screw, Brexit could be overturned altogether. From their perspective, it made a certain amount of sense – but from ours I could think of nothing more frightening. It had gone beyond the usual political shenanigans. This was a clear anti-democratic movement, being formed within the Westminster Parliament and supported from overseas.

We are supposed to put our faith and trust in Parliament to

deliver on our wishes at any given ballot. That's the whole nature of representative democracy: we mandate our politicians to do certain specific things, then on day-to-day matters we expect them to represent our interests in good faith. They might exercise a certain amount of judgement, but we have a reasonable moral expectation that they will do the things we explicitly elected them to do.

These were dark days. I spent many an hour poring over the news headlines, watching the late breaking news stories and reading the political commentary to look for any way forward. Nigel even went so far as to say that he felt it was the "darkest moment" he'd ever seen as an MEP or indeed in all his years fighting for Britain's independence.

During the October 'mini plenary' in Brussels, there was a debate on the preparation of the European Council sitting of October 17th-18th. The President of the Parliament, David Maria Sassoli, made a long and rather drawn-out statement. He admitted having met with John Bercow, who was then speaker of the House of Commons, just days prior:

"This morning I also had a fruitful meeting with the Speaker of the House of Commons John Bercow. I expressed my view to him that any request by the UK institutions to extend the withdrawal period should serve to give British citizens the floor - as this House said - by referendum or general election." - Sassoli, October 9th 2019

To put this into context, the President of the European Parliament was meeting with a man who had used almost every trick in the book to overturn the Brexit referendum outcome. I was sitting in front of Belinda de Lucy, MEP for South East England. She rose on a point of order, declaring that it was unacceptable for Sassoli to interfere so directly in Britain's domestic politics, exposing his intentions to intervene at all levels on behalf of the EU. It was Belinda's best speech, delivered with a calmness and clarity which exposed just how far the EU was prepared to go to deny the democratic decision of one of its own member states. Her expression reflected our indignation.

We will probably never know the exact nature of what was discussed between Sassoli and Bercow in that meeting. Given the 'temporary government' rumours which had been swirling around Westminster for months, I'm sure that I could hazard a guess as to the nature of it.

In the meantime, Jake Pugh and Robert Rowland had discovered Britain's liabilities with the European Investment Bank (EIB). When Britain joined the then European Economic Community, £3.5 billion was lodged with the EIB as part of our entry fee. The bank invests in long-term projects that are deemed to be safe – buildings, for example. That investment ensured that we owned roughly 16% of the bank, but because the EIB doesn't pay out dividends, as of 2020 our share is worth about £11 billion. The agreed Withdrawal Treaty between May's Government and the EU said that we would leave that money in the EIB.

There are two fundamental flaws with this foolish decision. Jake and Robert highlighted them quite clearly:

"Firstly, it is British taxpayers' money which our Government failed to protect in an international treaty

Secondly, and perhaps even more worryingly, our continued shared ownership of the EIB exposes us to the euro. Arguably, if the euro were to find itself in serious trouble, the EIB could request that the United Kingdom pay up to £37 billion to prop up a failing currency union within an organisation we had voted to leave."

This was a shocking piece of information which really highlighted to us just how awful the withdrawal treaty had been. We were still yet to see whether Boris Johnson would come back with any improvement. Some weeks later, Jake would tell me that he was on the Tube heading to Westminster where he bumped into Rishi Sunak, then Secretary to the Treasury. Jake informed Rishi about our EIB liabilities, which (according to Jake) came as news to Rishi. Jake surmised that Treasury mandarins had not fully briefed Rishi on this rather important detail. No-one can be expected to know all the intricacies of every international investment, but this one did seem rather a substantial omission which had a huge potential impact upon UK taxpayers. The lesson, if it needs spelling out, is obvious: without gaining full control of our own money, we wouldn't have properly left the European Union at all.

An offer was made to form a 'Leave Alliance' - a non-aggression pact between ourselves and the Tories to deliver a strong leave majority, and put to bed any talk of a second referendum or any further delay to the date when we would legally leave the EU. It was a fair offer, and one that many people supported.

There was a genuine fear, just as much as there had been during Theresa May's leadership, that a Remain alliance would come together to attempt to frustrate Brexit. Therefore, we had to do the same on our side of the argument. The ball was left in Boris Johnson's court, and we waited. In the meantime, the rumours of a Remain plot continued, and was widely reported. To what extent this was wishful thinking on the part of a Remain-supporting media, and to what extent the threat was genuine, is for others involved to reveal in time. It had one positive effect though: it hardened the resolve of Brexiteers of all persuasions to find a way forward.

Myself speaking at the Sedgefield rally September 11th 2019

CHAPTER 4 - Do or Die?

"Now we have to accept that we won't be able to leave on October 31st" - Sajid Javid MP

A shorter prorogation occurred without incident. Many people were surprised that when the Queen read out her annual speech to the House of Lords for the State Opening of Parliament on October 14th, very little was mentioned about Brexit. Either the desire was to de-politicise the address, given the events that had taken place, or perhaps the plan was to avoid giving any plans away, thus freeing the Government to pursue a way out of the EU by the looming deadline at the end of the month.

There was always going to be a major problem with the numbers in Parliament. It was Remain heavy. The Government had little credibility in the eyes of the public and there was still no agreement forthcoming – nor was there any certainty that one would actually materialise.

It arrived. Jacob Rees-Mogg touted it as a "fantastic and exciting deal". I sat in my Brussels office, waiting for it to be published. Like any reasonable person, I decided to reserve my judgement until the text was made available. We had heard the trumpeting of 'deals' before, and we weren't going to get too excited for fear of yet another disappointment. The announcement of the new Treaty was just three days after the Queen's speech, which proved that the decision not to talk too much about Brexit at the State opening had been a calculated move to allow for the fanfare of a new 'deal'.

Some hours later, I had the full text of the withdrawal agreement in front of me. I was disappointed to see no changes to the supremacy of the European Court of Justice, particularly on arbitration and the fact that their rulings could continue to apply to the United Kingdom even for years after transition.

Our fishing waters would still be governed under the EU fisheries policy during an extendable transition period, making it very difficult to prepare a UK fishing policy and to reach an amicable settlement with other nations after we had legally left the EU. The 'level playing field' provision on trade would still be in force in the Political Declaration (Paragraphs 17,77). That same paragraph 77 also obliged the UK to abide by EU rules on state aid - the same legislation that had prevented our Government from bailing out our steel industry.

Those points alone made many of us uneasy about this new 'fantastic' deal that Rees-Mogg had touted in Parliament. It wasn't Brexit as we had been arguing for, and it didn't make big enough changes to win our backing. There is no doubt it did change the Irish backstop provision, a change that even to this day I cannot see being a successful answer to the original poorly thought-out backstop - and one that may bring further political challenges for our own United Kingdom.

It was clear at this juncture that we had to fight to get a better deal - or if we could not, we should leave on World Trade Organisation terms. The political climate was also turning, and time was of the essence to get our point across.

Friday October 18th was the date for our rally in London, which had been originally intended as a sort of 'extension rebellion' – standing against the likelihood that Boris Johnson would be forced by the Benn Act to seek an extension to Article 50, trapping us in the European Union for a further three months. It was all beginning to seem a little like the Hotel California: you can vote out, but you can never leave. Those plans were quickly changed – the rally now presented an opportunity to voice our displeasure at the new 'deal'.

Nigel Farage was in a very different mood that evening in the 'green room'. I had arrived just in time for the start, having made a quick overnight turnaround from Brussels to Hartlepool and then down to the QE2 Centre in Westminster.

Nigel Farage points out the flaws in the Withdrawal Agreement at the QE2 Centre in London

Nigel was in a blue funk: very much not his usual ebullient self. I knew why. There was a Prime Minister who had made little change to the Withdrawal Agreement, potentially putting our relationship with Northern Ireland at risk. Ian Paisley Junior, the DUP MP for North Antrim since 2010, was also in the room. It became clear that the new Northern Ireland protocol would play a difficult part in the DUP's confidence agreement with the Conservatives.

Ian spoke with a sense of foreboding and concern about the direction of travel that Brexit appeared to be taking. This was a speech that did not necessarily resonate with every resident, but it struck a chord amongst the DUP faithful. His points were important to take on board. Nigel Farage followed to deliver one of the most difficult speeches of his political life. That speech was perhaps the most honest I'd ever heard from him. He was less bullish in his approach, keen to point out that the Government's new deal was in fact a new Treaty, bound by international law. It contained many elements which were unpalatable to himself and many Brexiteers.

Nigel's challenge was not to win over the crowd: they were already on his side. His challenge was to win the PR battle. The timing, so soon after Johnson's announcement of a new deal with Barnier and his team in Brussels, made it essential for Nigel to speak out. Otherwise, our chances would drain away.

It was proving more and more difficult to get the message across that no real significant changes had been made other than the removal of the backstop. Nigel is one of the very few politicians who has the ability to formulate a political argument and persuade many people to agree with him. This time he had to do it again, in the face of a concerted campaign by the Tory PR machine. Many of us as MEPs had to keep making the case for a better deal; and if none was forthcoming, we should simply trade on World Trade Organisation terms.

The clock was ticking. Just 13 days remained until the October 31st deadline. How could public opinion realistically change in such a short space of time, when almost all column inches were being taken up by front bench cabinet ministers singing the praises of their new Treaty with the EU? Even the opposition Labour MPs who wanted to stop Brexit were weighing in with arguments that gave the Remain case for a second referendum. That was unhelpful: not only did it gave extra weight to the Tory Party fanfare with their Brussels announcement, but it also helped the Tory whips to strong-arm their own backbenchers into voting for a sub-standard deal. We had an uphill battle to try to turn the tide of public opinion away from Boris' deal.

After Nigel had delivered his message to the rally at the QE2 Centre, social media, political commentators and many Brexiteers turned on him. Such was their belief that Boris' deal was in fact Brexit, they had turned on the Brexiteer-in-chief. Even columnist Rod Liddle referred to Anna Soubry's hatred of the deal as a reason to support its swift passage through the Commons.

Time was tight. A vote was scheduled for the following day, October 19th. It would be the first Saturday sitting of Parliament since April 1982 - following the Argentine invasion of the Falkland Islands. It was also the last possible day that Parliament could sit to debate and vote on the new Treaty to avoid asking for an extension to Article 50.

The order paper stated that the Government had put forward

two substantive motions offering options on whether the House would support the Withdrawal Agreement or support a no deal Brexit. Anyone who had been following the preceding three years since the referendum knew that the no-deal option would never pass the House. The key question in practice was whether or not the Government's preferred motion would pass. If not, all options – including a no-deal Brexit – remained very much on the table. It gave rise to the possibility that the new Treaty had a chance of passing the Commons stage before quickly being sent to the Lords, who were also sitting in anticipation.

Oliver Letwin is the sort of MP who has always divided opinion. He is a hero to Remain, and a thorn in the side of democracy to Brexiteers. He was the man who effectively made the vote on the 19th meaningless unless it supported the implementing legislation proposed by the Government. The Sun newspaper quoted a senior Tory "Letwin has gone and f***ed it again". Letwin was thrown out of the Tory Party a month earlier, having supported the Benn Act. Here he was, causing trouble for the Government again by proposing an amendment that demanded a vote on whether to accept the Government's proposal of three days of scrutiny before implementation.

There were, at the time, two ways of looking at these extraordinary events. If you were a Remain backer, you might have been thankful for Sir Oliver's input. If you were a Brexiteer and opposed Boris' Treaty, you might have breathed a sigh of relief. What mattered to Brexiteers then was that a General Election was painfully needed and that a 'Leave alliance', in which both the Brexit Party and Conservatives could agree not to stand against each other, should be established. The offer was consistently made to ensure Brexit happened. Again we waited.

I was in Strasbourg with colleagues at our dinner the evening of the vote on the implementing legislation after MPs had passed Johnson's Brexit Treaty. If MPs had passed the proposed three days of debate on the entire deal, we would be legally out of the European Union by the 31st – and we, as MEPs, would thankfully be out of a job. We could sense the PR battle slipping away from us, with time quickly running out. Rumour after rumour circled during the entire week leading up to that vote on the 22nd. If it confused us, and it was confusing MPs on all sides in the Houses of Parliament, it quite understandably also confused the public.

For the first time, I started to sense that something had changed. This deal was going to pass – not necessarily on that day, but some day. The Withdrawal Act had been passed by the Commons prior to the vote on the implementing legislation, with 322 votes in favour and 299 against.

Rumours abounded that Johnson would bring his deal forward again if he lost the vote on the implementing legislation. It was also suggested he would refuse to request an extension, echoing his 'do or die' pledge. The Tory press team did an amazing job of keeping their message simple. As long as the public believed Johnson was prepared to 'die in a ditch', it didn't matter whether an extension happened or not, because Parliament and the Labour Party would take the blame. Rumours that Boris Johnson might 'go to prison' rather than obey the Benn Act played straight into the government narrative – of a man doing his utmost to avoid an extension. If Boris had done everything humanly possible to get us out on October 31ˢᵗ, they reasoned, the public would blame Labour.

The battleground opened up. The implementing legislation failed to pass: 308 in favour, 322 against.

Boris now pulled his new Treaty back off the table. The only way to bring it back would be in a new session of Parliament – realistically, after a General Election.

The fight was now firmly on the territory where Boris Johnson wanted it. It was now clear that this had been their intention all along. The dividing lines were clear: the Conservatives painted themselves as wanting to 'get Brexit done', whilst Labour was the party dragging its heels, trying to force a second referendum. An election was looking inevitable. Messaging looked like it mattered more than Parliamentary votes.

Boris Johnson sent a letter requesting an extension of Article 50. To show that he was doing so only under duress, he did not sign it – and then sent a second letter, asking the EU to disregard the contents of the first letter. He signed the second one. The mood music was clear. Remainers howled in outrage: how dare our Prime Minister do such a thing as to try to obey the pledges on which he was elected?

The European Union wanted an extension. They ignored the covering letter, and granted the extension that Boris Johnson had 'requested', kicking Brexit back three months to the end of January.

Boris, reasoned many of the public, had tried as hard as he could. They could not blame him for failing in his 'do or die' pledge.

Behind the scenes: Dr. David Bull MEP with Nigel Farage at a public meeting

Chapter 5 - The Zombie Parliament

"Denying the electorate the chance of having its say this Parliament is a dead Parliament. It has no moral right to sit on these green benches" - *Geoffrey Cox MP*

Such was the zombie Parliament deadlock that the only way to resolve the Brexit issue was to call for a General Election. We had been making that point for many months, and we kept our offer of a Leave alliance on the table.

The Fixed-Term Parliaments Act was the obstacle which needed to be overcome. For an early General Election to take place, one of two conditions needed to be met – either:

• *A two-thirds majority in Parliament must vote to agree to an early General Election, or*

• *A motion of no-confidence passes in Her Majesty's Government, setting a 2-week countdown in motion - a General Election follows automatically, unless a government can be formed during that time which does enjoy the confidence of the House*

Theresa May had managed to get Parliamentary approval for her snap 2017 Election. Both Labour and the Conservatives were happy to agree to it. Now Boris was seeking to do the same. This time, though, the Parliamentary arithmetic was different. Dozens of backbench MPs had either defected or lost the whip. This had eroded Labour's numbers as well as the Conservatives'. These MPs knew that by voting for a General Election, they would lose their seats.

Labour MPs were jittery: since Boris Johnson had become Conservative leader, 50 opinion polls had been conducted by various companies. One, in July, had given Labour a 1% lead. The other 49 had given the Conservatives leads of up to 17%. Labour's MPs could not count upon the novelty factor of Jeremy Corbyn to bail them out as it had in 2017: his personal popularity had plummeted in the meantime. Labour did not want an election. It repeatedly called for an early election, then when the motion for an early election came to a vote, Labour abstained. MPs had voted by 298 to 56 at the start of September to call an early election. That might seem like a landslide, but it missed the two-thirds majority threshold.

Dull, dry statistics can't explain the level of farce. Parliament was trying to treat the Prime Minister as a puppet. It wouldn't allow him to govern. It wouldn't allow an election. It legislated to force him to request an EU extension. MPs routinely called for something, and then refused to vote for it.

On October 23rd, Frank Field and Sir Edward Leigh moved a motion to scrap the Fixed Term Parliaments Act. That, too, was defeated.

Boris Johnson responded by forcing his opponents to vote. If they wanted to scupper an election, they would now have to vote against rather than abstaining. He introduced a Bill to call an early election, which would get around the two-thirds majority issue.

The Liberal Democrats responded by producing a Bill of their own, with the intention of holding the General Election 72 hours earlier. The whole thing had grown incredibly petty. Day by day, public anger was growing. How could those who opposed Brexit dare say they wanted a 'people's vote' (a ridiculous phrase as the people had voted in droves in 2016), yet refuse to let the public decide who should form the government of the country? It was anti-democratic in the extreme.

Labour realised that the game was up. The government had the numbers to force an election this way. They had little choice but to support it, and the Bill calling for an early General Election was passed overwhelmingly by 438 to just 20 on October 29th. The Early Parliamentary General Election Act went through all its stages in a single day. An election would take place on December 12th. The game was on.

Richard Tice announces his candidacy for Hartlepool

Richard Tice announced his candidacy for my home constituency of Hartlepool on November 7th. This bombshell didn't come as any surprise to me. We'd had a private discussion in London following the candidates' rally at the Emmanuel Centre, a few days before. Hartlepool Council was now run by a Brexit Party-led coalition, so it seemed appropriate for his candidacy to be announced in the constituency along with the councillors who had joined the Brexit Party a month before.

I found myself stuck out in Brussels. We couldn't have all of our MEPs stand as Parliamentary candidates. Indeed, in the North East, there was a technical problem with doing it. If an MEP is elected to Westminster, they are required to resign as an MEP. The European elections are held on a closed-list voting system, so the next person down on the list steps up.

That's not usually a problem – but the North East is the smallest region in the country. We had only three MEPs, two of whom were Brexit Party. There was only one spare name on the list.

If Brian and myself had stood, and were elected, there would have been a vacancy in the European Parliament. Imagine a region-wide by-election to a European Parliament that we were due to leave: I would have been responsible for costing taxpayers literally millions of pounds unnecessarily.

I felt a bit like the 'designated survivor' in America, a politician who stays away from key events – making sure that in the event of a disaster, someone is available to keep the business of government going. It was my job to hold the fort in Brussels, and I hated being so far from the real action back home that I missed Richard Tice's press launch back home in the UK.

One of our local councillors in Hartlepool is the landlord of a local pub. Seeing a video of Richard pouring himself a pint at the Cosmopolitan on Hartlepool headland, I could sense his air of quiet confidence and touch of humour. Richard is not a man to take himself too seriously, and always displayed good-natured humour which certainly gave many activists a 'lift' in what would be a tough campaign in wintry and inclement weather.

The weeks leading up to the close of nominations gave us little time to decide how we would position ourselves in the campaign. We had to keep the message clear. Our offer of a Leave Alliance, where we could fight the Northern Labour seats that Conservatives had rarely, if ever, won, was still on the table. It was a fair offer, as it became clear that southern seats could be won by the Liberal Democrats if our vote split with the Conservatives. If the Conservatives stood in northern seats being targeted by us, this would potentially split the vote, helping Labour to keep its existing seats and even possibly make some gains. This put Brexit very much in jeopardy and we kept hammering home that clear danger. No offers were forthcoming from Tory HQ as the closing date for nominations was nearing.

I was sitting in our campaign office with colleagues when it was suddenly announced that Nigel Farage was coming to speak at the Grand Hotel in Hartlepool. Richard Tice, Brian Monteith and I were originally down to speak, but a last-minute change meant that only Nigel was to make an announcement. I had absolutely no inkling of what he was going to say.

"He's got the deal with the Tories"

"He's going to announce himself as a candidate"

I heard these, and many other, rumours swirling. I never have any faith in that kind of thing. It's the height of foolishness to trust political rumour – you'd be better off reading the tea leaves in the bottom of your cup: at least then you'd *know* it's nonsense.

The announcement that day shocked and divided many of us. Nigel told us that the Brexit Party would be stepping down in the 317 seats won by the Conservative Party in the 2017 General Election: we would not be responsible if they lost the election.

At the time, I wasn't sure whether or not this was the right decision. Some people refused to campaign, accusing us of having sold out to help a Tory Party Brexit deal they couldn't support. Some of those who had put hours of effort and finances into fighting their seats, only to be told at the last minute that they weren't going to be candidates, decided to stand as independents anyway.

Those 317 seats represented a lot of very disappointed former candidates, some of whom were sitting MEP colleagues in Brussels. The ever-present Alexandra Phillips, normally a staunch supporter of Nigel's, even tweeted to express her disappointment at being 'disenfranchised' and resolved that she would not be voting in the election at all. That day, there were a lot of highly-strung emotions and it changed the campaign irrevocably.

I didn't rock the boat. The decision had been made. What good could possibly come of me trying to fight against it? Nigel

Farage was our leader – and during an election campaign, you have to back your leader whether you agree with him or not. Nine times out of ten, ninety-nine times out of a hundred, I'm going to be fighting exactly the same corner as Nigel.

I'll tell you one thing about Nigel. He respects people who tell him to his face if they disagree with him, but he's scathing about those who whine to the press behind his back. In an Army, you don't question the General's orders. You obey. Sometimes, the General might be aware of a detail that a lower-ranked soldier doesn't know. The person who can see the full picture should make the decision.

Was it my favourite ever Nigel Farage decision? No – but I can respect the fundamental reasons why he made it. There was, as mentioned, still a possibility of another hung Parliament and that this time Remain would probably form a coalition of sorts to bring a second referendum to the table. It was perhaps just too risky to split the Brexit vote and achieve the opposite to what we had worked so hard for. On the other hand, a huge Tory majority was also possible. That would give Boris Johnson carte blanche to do whatever he wanted with regard to Brexit. Too risky.

By stepping down in the Conservative-held seats, Nigel would help them to prevent a Remain coalition – but not help them to win a landslide. If just a few Brexit Party MPs were elected, they might have disproportionate influence.

It was a unilateral decision. We stepped down in 317 seats for the good of the country. The Conservatives refused to step down in a single one. They merely demanded more. Would we, they wondered, please also step down in dozens of their top target seats? It was a case of giving them an inch, and them demanding a yard.

After bold announcement, the press went into overdrive. Conservative Central Office continued to hammer home further demands of us, to help them get a majority. That was a step too far. We weren't Tories. We'd already been more than fair in our decision not to contest the seats Conservatives won in 2017, and now they were asking for more. Some of our candidates were put under considerable personal pressure and eventually acquiesced; others bravely stood despite the mounting public pressure not to.

We had no problem with a bit of give-and-take, but the Conservatives expected us to do all the giving and them do all the taking. It reminded me a little bit of negotiations with the European Union...

There was even a concerted campaign by the Daily Mail to encourage the public to scare our remaining candidates into not standing and backing the Conservative candidate. The Mail even published the full list of email addresses of candidates, urging readers to contact them. Ann Widdecombe went on national television to reveal that she had been approached by Number 10 to ask her to step aside in return for favours. The election was underway. The dirty tricks campaign had begun.

Nigel turned up the heat. He accused some figures of essentially being corrupt: offering a peerage or seat at the negotiating table in return for stepping down . I wasn't approached myself, because I wasn't standing at the election, but many colleagues had expressed concerns over how they were being treated by the Conservatives. With that, we quickly rebuked their advances and vowed to fight on. The bitter aftertaste of their pressure was still in our mouths after close of nominations. We knew that the Conservatives and their supporters in the press were never going to make our lives easy. The responses on the doors in Hartlepool gave us very little reason to worry about whether we would at least get second place.

Richard Tice campaigns in Hartlepool

Sadly, however, events took over and made things much more difficult.

I was out knocking on doors with our canvassing team when I got a phone call from a supporter asking why four of our MEPs had left the Brexit Party. It was the first that I'd heard of it. Forman, [Annunziata] Rees-Mogg and Harris had resigned, joining Longworth who had the Party whip removed from him by Brian Monteith, our Chief Whip, only the day before. Brian knew something was about to happen but only had evidence of Longworth's intent – he couldn't discipline others and find he was being unjust – and possibly gain them sympathy. They would be christened the 'Gang of Four', a not-so-subtle reference to the breakaway Labour MPs who had formed the SDP in the early 1980s.

We had known privately for a while that Forman and Longworth were becoming less and less active or even supportive of the Brexit Party, often writing against Brexit Party official policy. It was, however, a surprise to me to see all four do this on the same day. To cross the floor when a party has fundamentally changed its nature is one thing. I can't blame ex-Ukippers for leaving when their party lurched in a vastly different direction to the platform they were elected on. I can't fault ex-Labour MPs who resigned or defected over the anti-Semitism which pervaded their party. But this was something different altogether. The Brexit Party had remained rock-solid in its support for Brexit, and gone above and beyond the call of duty in stepping down in so many seats. And the timing – to resign, not just in a co-ordinated fashion, but during a General Election campaign!

This felt like the ultimate betrayal: a stabbing in the front, more akin to Brutus delivering the fatal blow to Caesar on the floor of the Senate.

Looking back, I still feel aggrieved that they resigned. In so doing, they damaged the campaign further. All four of them are talented individuals and doubtless are ambitious. I hold no ill will towards them: they made their decision, and despite the disappointing news we soldiered on. We kept the campaign in Hartlepool going and put all our efforts into speaking to as many voters as possible right up to the close of the polls.

Their resignations didn't seem to have much effect on the doors. I remember just one person raising the resignations as a reason not to vote for us. It seemed to me that we could turn the tide of disappointment.

How wrong we were! What happened just days later shocked, sickened and surprised the Party and all our campaigners. David Mincher was a former UKIP councillor, elected to everyone's surprise in May 2019. He had been checked and vetted before being admitted to the Brexit Party. There had been no indication of the kind of views he would later express. Nothing would prepare us for the shocking revelations that came to our attention after Channel 4 contacted us with undercover footage of racism.

We knew immediately who that undercover person was. Hindsight is a wonderful thing but you develop a sense for those who are genuine and those who are not. This gentleman wore the Brexit Party rosette and offered to campaign in the hours off his 'seasonal work', having come up from somewhere down South. I think I spoke with him for about 2 minutes, and he asked a lot of questions. I'm always on my guard when people ask too many questions. Remember, politics is an arrogant business. It sticks out like a sore thumb when someone has so many questions. What, I wondered, was the angle here? It was easily forgotten in the heat of the moment: if I spoke out every time something felt a little unnerving, I'd never stop speaking out. I made a mental note to be careful what I said to him, and thought no more of it at a time when everything was so totally focused upon the campaign.

A few days later, I was sorting out the campaign office for the next day with a couple of the team. The email from Channel 4 came through.

I remember kicking a pile of leaflets I'd just sorted. I might even have let out a few expletives. Our campaign manager, who was with us, just dropped his shoulders. I knew exactly how he felt. You try hard to build a team, hone your campaign strategy and get people motivated. Not this time. We'd worked day in day out, hours at a time, knocking on as many doors as possible to build a rapport with those we were seeking to represent. What Mincher did was beyond the pale. It would cause huge damage to the campaign through absolutely no fault of our own. One man's foul point of view should never represent an entire Party, but the damage was irreparable. Many media reports tainted the Party with the same brush as Mincher's awful opinions. That's bang out of order in my view. The test of a party isn't whether it has bad eggs, but whether it disciplines them and kicks them out so fast that their feet don't touch the floor. That's what UKIP did so well under Nigel's leadership – and when it stopped kicking those people out later, that's when the rot set in. On the Left of politics, the difference in approach between Jeremy Corbyn and Keir Starmer on such matters is immense.

We took no time in removing Mincher from the Brexit Party, and he would eventually resign from the Council. Now began the effort of putting the campaign back together. Brexit Party members and supporters from all over the country came to help on huge action days. It was a case of damage limitation, trying to turn the tide of the campaign back onto the issue of Brexit.

There is no doubt in my mind that a good 20-25% of those who voted Tory on election day were originally going to vote for us. To this day I'm convinced we would have finished in at least a respectable second place had the ugly remarks from Mincher never been made. Politics isn't just about what you hear on the doorstep. It's also about momentum, building the idea of being successful and moving from strength to strength. The scandal itself isn't what hurts, it's the way that it distracts attention from the positive message you're trying to get across. Getting back on track, getting people to listen again, that's the difficult part.

The final week of the campaign was upon us. The plan was clear: to try and keep as many of our pledges as possible on-side to give ourselves a fighting chance.

We rolled out the big gun. Nigel Farage came to Hartlepool right up to the final day before polls opened. People came from far and wide to help with our polling day operation and it felt optimistic.

June Mummery and Nigel converse before campaigning in Hartlepool

Work on the morning of December 12th began at 5am. I wouldn't get to bed until gone 4:30am the next day, almost a full 24 hours with barely a chance to catch my breath. Polling days are exhausting in politics. It was the same for many of the activists who gave their time and efforts so valiantly.

Our canvassing efforts throughout the campaign (with relatively few day-to-day activists outside of our action days) meant we had covered roughly three-quarters of the constituency, with many Labour voters switching to us due to Corbyn's lack of support for Brexit. Their steadfast refusal to bring themselves to vote for the Tories meant we could expect between 20-30% of the vote on the day. The challenge lay in convincing the more conservative voters to switch as well. Often, that boiled down to the chance of success: if they believe you're going to win, they'll switch their votes. If not, they'll vote Conservative anyway – another reason why momentum is so important.

We had worked our proverbials off in those areas that would traditionally vote Conservative to squeeze their vote and believed we had managed to do well. Of course, the Channel 4 story had set us back - now it was just a case of finding out by how much.

Throughout the campaign, much fanfare was made of Boris Johnson's "let's get Brexit done" strapline and there's no doubt that that strategy had worked very well. Since stepping aside in the 317 seats the Conservatives had won in 2017, our poll ratings for us had slipped. If you step aside in half the seats, your national share of the vote will halve even if your support holds up nationally. The problem is that as the numbers go down for that reason, it creates a perception that the Party is slipping – and that perception leads to people believing that the Party can't win, who then switch their votes elsewhere. The national picture was not great for us, but in some seats we held out some hope and kept on going.

I could see the ballot boxes being emptied at the count. Areas of Hartlepool that you'd never expect to vote Tory in a million years were showing a significant Conservative vote. Within the first hour or so, a select few of us knew that it was only a battle for second place between ourselves and the Conservatives. Labour would win the seat, but not by very much. By the time Richard walked into the counting room, we had prepared ourselves for the fact we'd come third. It was a bitter pill to swallow. The Conservatives never stood a chance of winning in Hartlepool, but a strong Tory vote prevented us from doing so.

Events, dear boy, events – that's the famous Harold Macmillan quote. Our campaign in Hartlepool had been completely scuppered by events. In the end, our vote was squeezed through fear that Labour might have won the election nationally.

It would be wrong of me not to mention the many good, decent and hardworking people who gave their all in the campaign: mostly young and passionate Brexiteers who gave up their time to campaign and try to win the Hartlepool constituency. I don't think words are enough to express my own gratitude, and I know that Richard feels the same. After the election, I asked Richard if he'd do it all again and whether he had any regrets. He didn't hesitate for a moment: there were no regrets at all, and he would do it all over again.

With the benefit of hindsight, many people change their minds and wish they'd done things differently. They second-guess themselves and their decisions. Not so Richard: he knew that we had done our utmost in incredibly trying circumstances. It is not often that a brand-new party makes such a strong showing at a General Election campaign with little time to prepare, reduced resources, limited manpower and very little airtime. We faced a very well-oiled Tory election machine in full swing, during the depths of winter.

When you look at it like that, I'd say we did pretty damn well.

To this day, there are still some commentators who blame the Brexit Party for stopping the Conservatives from making further gains. On the one hand, you could accuse them of being greedy, but in my opinion they have missed the real effect the Brexit Party had on the campaign.

Put aside the seats in which we stepped aside. Look closely at where the Tories won surprising victories in 'red wall' seats such as Blyth Valley and Redcar. The Brexit Party wasn't taking Conservative votes in those seats. It was attracting traditional Labour voters from among those who would never vote Conservative, pulling away enough votes from Labour to open up the chance of a Conservative victory. Blyth Valley is a classic example of this: in 2017, the Conservatives were in second place with Labour some 8000 votes ahead; in 2019, the Tory vote only increased by almost 2000 votes. It was Labour voters turning to the Brexit Party who ensured that an increase of just 5.8% for the Tories gave them a seat in which they had been almost 20% behind in 2017.

There are plenty more examples of this phenomenon. In Sedgefield, my colleague David Bull fought valiantly to reduce

Labour's vote share. The Tories took Tony Blair's former seat in a national shock. Would they have done so without the Brexit Party acting as a safety valve to cream off some Labour votes? I'm not sure they would. Burnley, North-West Durham and Don Valley also fell – and again, the Brexit Party probably enabled that. Labour leadership hopeful Laura Pidcock and long-time stalwart Caroline Flint both lost their seats. Wakefield, Bury North, Delyn, Heywood and Middleton – the list is so long.

My emotions, like everyone else's, were running all over the place after that election result. We were devastated not to have made Brexit Party gains, yet we knew that Brexit – at least in some form – would definitely now happen. In the process, a few key concessions had been extracted from Boris Johnson. There was disappointment, yes, but we also had something we could take to the bank.

FACTS AND FIGURES

One of the biggest criticisms which was levelled at the Brexit Party is the claim that we somehow 'endangered Brexit' by contesting the General Election at all. I don't believe that's the case- far from it!

We certainly didn't stop the Conservatives from holding their own seats, because we'd stepped down in them. As for the marginals, well...the facts certainly tell a story!

Remember that across the country, this was the situation:

The national picture

	PARTY	VOTE SHARE	% CHANGE
	Conservative	43.6%	1.2%
	Labour	32.1%	-7.9%
	Lib Dem	11.6%	4.2%

We see that across the country as a whole, the Labour vote went down substantially. The Liberal Democrat vote increased. There was only a small increase in vote share for the Conservative Party, but they were still able to win the election with a large 80-seat majority.

Let's take a look at what happened in Labour's so-called 'red wall'.

In seats where the Brexit Party stood, we find an unexpected effect. Blyth Valley had always been a Labour seat...until now:

Blyth Valley result 2019

	PARTY	VOTE SHARE	% CHANGE
	Conservative	42.7%	5.8%
	Labour	40.9%	-15.0%
	Brexit Party	8.3%	8.3%
	Lib Dem	5.3%	0.7%
	Green	2.8%	0.6%

Despite a decent showing for the Brexit Party, we see that the Conservative vote increased by far more than the national average.

Meanwhile, Labour's collapse was spectacular. Remember that the Conservatives had *never* won this seat at any point in history - until this election, when the Brexit Party stood.

Can anyone honestly claim that the Brexit Party damaged the Conservatives here?

Sedgefield is a town in the North East of England with a long history of coal mining. It's known for being Tony Blair's former constituency. In the 1990s, Labour took over 70% of the vote here. Nobody would have possibly imagined them losing such a safe seat just a few years earlier. This is what happened...

Sedgefield result 2019

	PARTY	VOTE SHARE	% CHANGE
	Conservative	47.2%	8.4%
	Labour	36.3%	-17.1%
	Brexit Party	8.5%	8.5%
	Lib Dem	4.7%	2.8%
	Green	2.4%	0.7%
	Independent	0.9%	0.9%

The pattern here is even more striking. The Labour Party didn't just dip below 50% of the vote, it turned a majority of under 6,000 into a Conservative majority of over 4,500. So where did the Brexit Party vote come from, if not from Labour?

Remember that UKIP only took 4.2% in 2017, so most of the Brexit vote clearly did not come from UKIP. Again, the Brexit Party didn't harm the Conservatives one bit here!

The Labour Party had held the seat of Don Valley for almost a century, winning it comfortably enough even in Conservative landslide election victories. What a coincidence that Labour just happened to lose for the first time in 2019 - the very same year that the Brexit Party entered the fray!

Don Valley result 2019

	PARTY	VOTE SHARE	% CHANGE
	Conservative	43.2%	1.5%
	Labour	35.2%	-17.8%
	Brexit Party	13.7%	13.7%
	Lib Dem	4.2%	2.3%
	Green	1.9%	1.9%
	Yorkshire Party	1.8%	-1.7%

The Conservative Party didn't do anything special here. Its vote increased by 1.5%, in keeping with the 1.2% national average.

But the Brexit Party's 13.7% destroyed any chance Labour might have had of holding the seat. Labour's collapse was dramatic, and the Brexit Party's vote couldn't have come from UKIP (they didn't even stand at the previous election).

The Welsh constituency of Delyn shows the same effect, but in a completely different type of seat. Delyn doesn't fit the pattern of being a Labour 'red wall' seat, but the Brexit Party was no friend of Labour here either.

Delyn result 2019

	PARTY	VOTE SHARE	% CHANGE
	Conservative	43.7%	2.6%
	Labour	41.4%	-10.8%
	Lib Dem	6.1%	3.5%
	Brexit Party	5.1%	5.1%
	Plaid Cymru	3.7%	-0.1%

Delyn is a Labour-leaning marginal seat. The Conservatives only won it in their landslide years of 1983 and 1987. If the Brexit Party was going to hurt the Conservatives anywhere, it would be in a constituency like Delyn.

The Brexit Party's effect was more modest here, but still the Conservatives outperformed their national vote share and Labour suffered a greater decline than expected. The presence of the Brexit Party was at worst neutral for the Conservatives - and arguably, it cost Labour the seat.

Our last example is the traditional Labour working-class town of Burnley. Nobody would have given the Conservatives a chance of winning it - that is, before the events of 2019 and the introduction of the Brexit Party to politics.

Burnley result 2019

	PARTY	VOTE SHARE	% CHANGE
	Conservative	40.3%	9.4%
	Labour	36.9%	-9.9%
	Lib Dem	9.0%	-6.0%
	Brexit Party	8.6%	8.6%
	BAPIP	3.0%	3.0%
	Green	1.9%	0.8%
	Independent	0.3%	0.3%

Burnley had been Labour since 1935 until the Liberal Democrats won it in 2010. Even the collapsing Liberal Democrat vote couldn't save the Labour Party here, and the Conservative vote share increased dramatically. Remember - their vote went up by 1.2% nationally, so a 9.4% rise in Burnley was eye-catching. A solid Brexit Party performance didn't prevent their success. Far from it! If anything, the Brexit Party were responsible for stopping Labour.

I haven't cherry-picked these examples. There are so many other constituencies across the country where the same pattern is repeated. Perhaps there would have been a different story if the Brexit Party had stood in traditional Conservative areas, but it was a strategic decision not to do so.

The Brexit Party acted responsibly in the 2019 General Election campaign. Indeed, far from jeopardising the Conservatives' chances, sometimes I wonder whether we accidentally did them *too much* of a favour! With Boris Johnson sitting on an 80-seat majority in Parliament, he has a little too much free rein - and little to fear from his own more eurosceptic backbench MPs.

Perhaps you think it's a little strange that I've devoted quite so much space to a single argument, but it's often these claims which are the most damaging ones in politics. The notion of 'country before party' is part of the DNA of those of us who campaigned for the Brexit Party. I was a Member of the European Parliament for just seven months. I didn't want to be there any longer than I had to.

We made decisions in good faith, based upon the information available to us at the time. Even with hindsight, I believe the evidence shows we made the correct decision far more often than we made a mistake.

Any claim that we acted recklessly could not be further from the truth.

Chapter 6 - The calm after the storm

"I killed the Liberal Democrats and I hurt the Labour Party" – Nigel Farage

Strasbourg in December is a city to behold. I highly recommend it for a long weekend (do avoid the mid-week when the European Parliament is sitting – hotel prices at least double) to experience the truly unique Christmas markets and atmosphere.

Strasbourg self-identifies as 'the capital of Christmas', and anyone who's spent time walking down the cold streets, a cup of mulled wine in hand, wandering by the river, enjoying the music and traditional decor, browsing through the Christmas market, will understand completely why they do it. To me it was always a city of two halves: the traditional, with its glorious cathedral and old-fashioned restaurants, contrasting with the functional grey insides of the Parliament buildings.

I made it to Strasbourg a day early to avoid the Monday madness of making the journey and it allowed me a chance to catch up on much-needed sleep. The European Parliament is a very quiet place on a Monday morning, a surreal calm before the storm. Everyone knew at this point that the Brexit deal agreed in October was going to get through the Commons in January and the general approach from the Parliament was that they would rubber-stamp the Commission proposal. We knew we would be out at the end of January, so it was a perfect time to really get into the Christmas spirit - and boy did we have a fun week!

Every Tuesday evening in Strasbourg we would all have dinner together at a brilliant restaurant in the Jewish quarter of the city. Our Chief Whip, Brian Monteith, had decided we would take part in a Secret Santa. Bearing in mind we were a group of about 40 or so people, MEPs and staff colleagues all took part in handing out our presents. Some presents were considerably risqué - and only those present will know what I am talking about. Plenty of wine was flowing, party hats were worn, and I think we left the restaurant staff with a fair amount of cleaning up to do. I have a very good inkling as to who bought my secret Santa – but *that's a secret I'll always keep to myself.*

Brian Monteith (Chief Whip) with our flags

Looking back at that evening and the many bars we visited following our meal, I have to say it was the most enjoyable evening I'd had in years - let alone during the seven months we'd all been thrown together since our huge election win in May 2019. There was a palpable sense of relief that whilst the election had not gone so well for our Party, we knew we had done our utmost to stop a second referendum and all of us were in agreement that our own WTO Brexit position was effectively still on the table. After a proxy victory in the General Election, we celebrated the defeat of the Remain parties as well as our own individual efforts in fighting to unshackle the Brexit deadlock.

Nursing several hangovers the following day didn't matter a jot to us. We'd had uproarious fun and further cemented our friendships. For the rest of that week, we continued to support each other in the Parliament chamber and there was a noticeable difference in the attitudes of those who respected or even supported our political battle and of those who vehemently opposed us. Politicians from various parts of Europe frequently came up to us to congratulate us on playing a significant part in securing the referendum result in 2016, and we felt very humbled by their encouraging words both privately and publicly. Those who opposed us would ignore us and bury their heads in the sand. I was told that one Labour MEP even refused to let one of our MEPs share a car to the Parliament. There is a sense of self-respect in losing graciously. Others couldn't bring themselves to even begrudgingly admit defeat. Britain was going to have its Brexit day, and we looked forward to moving on.

After such a gruelling election campaign, the Christmas break couldn't come soon enough. I needed it more than I can ever remember, and taking time to breathe and unwind with family was precisely the sort of recuperation that everyone needed before our final month as MEPs and Britain's final month as a legal member of the European Union.

Yes, the Treaty was not necessarily to our liking and we had campaigned for a better one but it was very hard to see how that could be achieved when you had little time and your mandate would come to an end. The Conservatives had achieved a majority the likes of which had not been seen since Mrs. Thatcher's win in the 1980s. The 'red wall' was crumbling in the North and with such a clear mandate in support of 'getting Brexit done', the democratic outcome had to be respected.

Christmas could not have come at a better time. I spent the festive period reflecting on a crazy year from my perspective. At no point had I ever expected to be elected to the European Parliament, meet such an exciting array of individuals from all walks of life, build strong friendships, be part of an exciting movement that got rid of one of the most duplicitous Prime Ministers in recent times and go through a gruelling and cold winter General Election in 2019.

If anyone had told me that that would be my 2019, I'd have said they were certifiable. *But then, I could hardly have predicted my 2020 either...*

Chapter 7 - Flag-gate

"My flag is not a glass of water!"

– Brian Monteith

That first week back in Brussels after New Year was one of mixed emotions. I knew what was ahead, and was looking forward to seeing out my final month as an MEP, but I knew that my staff were facing the more immediate reality of losing their jobs. This was a time to let them plan their next moves. I would not ask too much of them work wise other than the basic day-to-day administration, take them out for lunch and allow them a little more freedom, knowing their job was going to be no more in a matter of weeks.

The main crux of our predicament was how we intended to vote on the final Withdrawal Agreement. Some were keen to vote in favour and some were opposed. We wrangled over various pros and cons and this would go on right up to the vote itself, but more on that later.

Our final Strasbourg session of the European Parliament was one that had a very different feeling about it, and it had nothing to do with the fact it was our last visit to the city. It had more to do with how people across the Parliament acted towards us. They were so approachable - there was none of the air of hostility that we'd felt in the preceding months. It was an air of final acceptance. It was the final stage of grief. The European Union Withdrawal Bill had passed the Commons and that was that. There was no real prospect of the European Parliament as a whole voting against the Withdrawal Agreement as it had been a negotiated agreement between the Commission and the British Government. The European Parliament has rarely voted down a Commission proposal, save during the furore over the Santer Commission in 1999, in reaction to the allegations of Edith

Cresson's financial impropriety. So we had to resolve whether we could use our vote to make a final political statement. Either way it would be a political statement because it would be our final act, our final task before we went back to our lives and lost our MEP suffix.

There was one more surprise in store for us from the Parliamentary authorities. I was sitting with my colleagues, ready to take part in various votes in the Strasbourg session. We'd go into the chamber armed with lengthy voting lists which we'd discussed with colleagues and advisors in detail to make sure that we all knew what we were voting on, and why. I never experienced the worst of it: some weeks towards the end of a Parliament, MEPs would vote upwards of a thousand times in a single week. There are so many votes that, ironically, it becomes harder to ensure democratic accountability? How can you possibly understand the nuances of every single one of them? We had to trust staff to advise us, trust colleagues from the relevant committees, and then form a judgement together.

For decades, there had been a simple tradition: that British eurosceptic MEPs would put a simple desk flag in front of them, as a simple reminder that we're there to represent our national interest. Other countries' MEPs, from a variety of political groups, would follow suit. You'd see the occasional regional flag too. It was one of the few bits of character in an otherwise soulless chamber.

This had been going on for twenty years, but in our last month, five minutes into the session, the ushers came to remove our flags – at the behest of the President of the Parliament.

It felt like a completely unnecessary display of political childishness, but we could not be surprised. The timing seemed deliberate: one final insult to the eurosceptics in the European Parliament. Quite frankly, it beggared belief. The leader of a different Parliamentary Group (we had chosen not to join a pan-national grouping) rose on a point of order to question why the President had made such a decision unilaterally, without even communicating it to members of the Parliament. It was hardly democratic.

A Liberal Democrat MEP spoke up, leaping to the European Parliament's defence – pointing out, in all seriousness, that glasses of water aren't permitted on desks either (of course, the reason why a glass of water isn't allowed is that they don't want water to spill on the electronic voting equipment or microphones – a small table flag is perfectly safe).

Brian Monteith, my fellow North East MEP and also our Chief Whip, decided that it was time to intervene. Instead of simply pointing out the ludicrous inconsistency of the Liberal Democrat intervention, he bellowed out the words which I'll never forget:

"My flag is not a glass of water!"

The mix of seriousness and humour defused a bit of tension – some MEPs from across the political spectrum stood in unison and applauded. It revealed a very fundamental reality of the way the EU generally perceives nation states. The pathetic banning of national flags was and is a clear indicator that the EU is not interested in nation states and in fact wishes to supersede them.

If I needed a poignant reminder to symbolise why we needed to leave – finally – on January 31st, I'd got it. Brian's words have forever become etched in the psyche of the former Brexit Party MEPs. Whenever we meet in the future, the immortal words "My flag is not a glass of water" will forever be his badge of honour.

Brian Monteith addresses the chamber

It was time for a spirited response. Thus, Martin Daubney (without filling us all in on his plan in advance) began 'Operation Liberate Union Jack'. The Parliamentary Secretariat was incredulous when they turned up one day, only to find that the Union Jack had disappeared from the array of 28 European national flags. They had no idea who had removed it, or indeed how long it had been missing.

The European Parliament may have taken our flags – but now Martin had liberated one of theirs in response. He'd hatched a plan to take the Union Jack flag from the Strasbourg Parliament and repatriate it back home to the United Kingdom, having its very own miniature Brexit.

Martin Daubney discreetly removes the flag

I didn't know what to think – was it a good idea, a courageous display of defiance against the European Union? Or was it a little childish prank that wasn't needed so close to Brexit Day –

and might well land Martin in hot water? We were all scratching our heads a little, but we certainly admired the sheer audacity of it all.

Martin knew he had to own up to it. Sooner or later, they'd probably have found him out from the security footage anyway. It was a little fun, some free publicity when the Sun newspaper broke the story. The cat was out of the bag, and we waited to see what would happen next.

"So much anger welled up inside me over the flag ban that we decided to liberate our flag. We called it Operation Liberate Jack" – Martin Daubney.

Social media went into overdrive. Like Watergate, Deflategate, Weinergate, and many others including the obvious Gate-gate, this deserved a name. Operation Liberate Jack was christened Flag-Gate.

Supporters and opposition alike had plenty to say, but nothing really fazed Martin. He's what you'd expect of a former lads' mag editor - very much your cheeky chappie, the sort of person who enjoys being both hero and villain, and he wore that moniker well during his time in Brussels. The whole thing had an air of the daring and it was all done in good humour rather than with any kind of malice. I count myself particularly fortunate to have been a colleague of his and there was many an evening spent over a beer or three where I heard the tales of his former life as editor of Loaded magazine.

Rumours abounded over what would happen once the Parliament found out. I never found out – perhaps they just decided it wasn't worth making an issue of, so close to Brexit Day. Even for them, discretion can sometimes be the better part of valour. Perhaps this episode is something that will be remembered as a daring and surprising act that showed the sheer chutzpah of the man. How did he get away with it? Didn't someone see him taking the flag down? What had happened in the President's office? Where is the flag today? It's a mystery that only Martin himself knows, but I for one applaud the audacity and symbolism of flag-gate.

So ended our final Strasbourg Parliamentary session. It was a strange feeling to leave the city for the final time and I afforded myself a final bière before embarking on the journey home with June Mummery, Christina Jordan, Jake Pugh, Claire Fox and Ben Habib. I slept for almost the whole trip back.

Always good to be heading home!

Chapter 8 - The Brexit door

"The end of the road: a 47-year political experiment the British have frankly never been very happy with"

– Nigel Farage

Those final two weeks in Brussels were the oddest of my life. They were a sort of limbo: counting down the days to our national freedom and our own unemployment. You'll hear eye-watering tales of how much money MEPs who'd served for decades would get in severance pay, but the reality for the newly-elected MEPs was that we didn't get a penny. Fine! I've never been one for avarice.

Nigel Farage leaves the Parliament Chamber for the last time, flanked by Martin Daubney and Michael Heaver

**Nigel faces the cameras
after the historic vote**

We had two things to do: firstly, to tie up the loose ends. There were offices to be closed down, goodbyes to be said, and important documents to be shredded (well no, not the last one – we'd never done anything that needed to be hidden). I spent a wonderful afternoon with my two assistants and some colleagues over a long lunch halfway into the penultimate week. The venue had been recommended to me by a staffer who had lived in Brussels for many years. I liked the authenticity of the place. The food was passable, and more to the point, it had a very extensive drinks menu. Perfect. If memory serves correctly, we started at around midday and finished around

6pm. I remember the relaxed conversations and general laissez-faire attitude, a perfect foil to the many weeks and months of political war-gaming that had passed.

We had one simple rule for that afternoon: 'no politics'.

June Mummery, Ben Habib and Christina Jordan celebrate

The second task was of much more fundamental importance. It was about legacy, and I was still very much in two minds. We needed to decide how we intended to vote on the Withdrawal Agreement. As a democrat, I had to respect the majority that our voters had given the British Government and the confidence they had in their 'get Brexit done' slogan. It seemed that the minutiae of the agreement was not up for discussion. Richard Tice reminded us that it was the Brexit Party who had secured the commitment from Boris Johnson that he would not seek an extension to the transition period. I reminded myself of the Strasbourg evening when we celebrated the failure of Remain, their failure to secure a second referendum and the fact that if talks failed during transition and Boris was true to his word, our Party position of trading on WTO terms was still on the table.

There was still a problem though. The sums of money were now lower, but we still had to pay the so-called 'divorce bill' which went way beyond our legal obligations. There was far too much keeping the UK tied in to the European Union. Although some of the language had been softened since Theresa May's deal, there were many areas which could potentially be used to keep the UK tied down to the European Union. A lot would depend on the future: could we trust Boris Johnson to look out for our own interests in the future relationship negotiations? Were we, in effect, writing a blank cheque?

I also had reservations as to whether the Government, with such a large majority and a weak opposition on the Labour benches, would be prepared to walk away from talks. They were no longer fearful of their own ERG backbenchers, because they didn't need to rely upon them for their majority. Did it have the guts, if necessary, to accept (in effect) a no-deal Brexit on December 31st 2020?

I did the right thing. I war-gamed all three possibilities: voting in favour, voting against, and abstaining. I rejected abstaining very quickly. It would be seen as weak, as a cop-out, failing to engage with the very reason that we were there in the first place. So I prepared statements supporting both positions, speaking them both and trying them out for size against each other. Which of these did I feel more comfortable with? Which was the correct legacy?

Someone leaked the statements. To the Guardian. That was the start of my final week in Brussels. No matter! After, all Boris Johnson himself allegedly prepared two statements in support of and against Leave before finally deciding to campaign for Leave in the referendum.

The thought that I shouldn't have weighed up both sides fully and fairly before making such a momentous decision? Absolute madness. Of course it was right for me to give careful consideration to both ways of voting – and on a point of principle, I was definitely not abstaining on the issue I had campaigned for all of my adult life.

The beginning of that final week, the atmosphere in the Parliament and responses from so many people was one of a final sense of acceptance - the final stage in the five stages of grief.

There was a lot of agonising for the Brexit Party MEPs. An hour before the debate in the chamber, we met for our last ever voting meeting. Some voices spoke up, arguing passionately that the Withdrawal Agreement was not Brexit. Others spoke up, arguing that there was one inescapable fact: this was the only deal on the table. The Brexit Party had secured a commitment from the Prime Minister that he would not seek an extension to the transition period. By voting for this Agreement, we knew that the possibility of a real Brexit, of true freedom, was kept alive. It was clear to us that the Parliament would vote in favour. We knew that our votes on this were not going to be pivotal. The question was simple: what was the right thing to do? The Commission would get its way, regardless of what we chose to do. Voting against wouldn't make a jot of difference to the final outcome.

There were voices on both sides in the meeting, a furious debate. There were two things we had to avoid: abstentions (it would be awful for the Brexit Party to abstain on Brexit), and disunity (voting in different directions).

It was a tense meeting, but a productive one. We resolved to support the vote with some deep reservations. We could not in all conscience reject Brexit, nor indeed ignore the fact that the British voter had given their backing to Boris' election pledge of 'Get Brexit Done' and his commitment not to extend the transition period. These were victories that would not have happened had it not been for the Brexit Party. We weren't going to be the people to spoil the party and go back to the days of Parliamentary tricks and spin.

Nigel Farage would give his final speech in the European Parliament. The Parliament tries to 'push' parties into joining a European Parliamentary grouping. Because we hadn't, our speaking time was severely limited. That meant that normally members of our group would get a minute. Sixty seconds for Nigel to say goodbye just seemed pathetically insufficient. Brexit Party MEPs who thought Nigel deserved far more than that chose to give him our own speaking time, so he was able to take the full four minutes allocated to us. And what a four minutes it was!

The world's media covered every moment of that final debate. In fact, journalists filled almost every available space in our part of the chamber. As Nigel signed off for the last time, we waved our flags. It was a final act of defiance against the recent rule change, but more importantly it would signify our nation's return to self-governance. Mairead McGuinness, the Irish MEP, was presiding over the session. She cut off Nigel as he finished, then she signed off by saying "Put your flags away. You're leaving and take them with you". We did so gladly – and after the debate, we headed over to the 'Mickey Mouse' bar (fondly known as such because of the cartoon-type feel to the furniture, not just because it's in a Mickey Mouse Parliament with no real power) which is next to the Parliament chamber in Brussels to celebrate this historic moment.

I was wearing a Union Jack tie and pocket square, as was James Wells. Jonathan Bullock went a step further, wearing Union Jack socks. We all had so many memories of the most extraordinary seven months of our lives. We were just minutes away from the vote, deep in conversation, when our chat was rudely interrupted by the division bell. Time to make history!

We rushed back to the chamber to vote for the final time. Emotions were running high and many of us were looking forward to new future away from Brussels. I couldn't actually believe that I was contributing to the final decision on Britain's membership of the EU, after having campaigned for our nation's independence all of my adult life.

I found myself at my seat, with a voting list before me that read:

"Agreement on the withdrawal of the United Kingdom of Great Britain and Northern Ireland from the European Union and the European Atomic Energy Community"

I could scarcely believe it. To be in that position, to press the button that would seal the United Kingdom's exit from the European Union, is the stuff that dreams are made of. I can't say that I had any movie-style moment where my whole life flashed before my eyes, but I can tell you just how emotional that moment was. I was voting on something that I'd fought so hard for, for so many years in the face of abuse, lost friendships and relationships.

I didn't believe that this was a good deal. However delighted I was that we were leaving, there was the immense sadness at having to vote in favour of such a flawed deal. Politics means compromises, having to make a binary choice in a world that is far more complex than that. This was the only deal on the table. Nigel Farage had secured a commitment from Johnson that he would not extend the transition period beyond the agreed December 31st 2020. That was the tipping point for me. Both myself and many colleagues were moved to have been there to see the day Britain legally left the EU.

I thought of the many thousands who worked hard to achieve this momentous result, especially those who are no longer with us. They were the ones who had given their last £5 of pension money, the people who had delivered leaflets in all weathers to build the movement before it became popular. I was saddened that many of them didn't live to see the moment when our freedom came back to us.

As an unmarried man, it's probably safe for me to describe it as the most emotional moment of my life. It was an incredible, euphoric feeling – yet with a touch of the bittersweet, knowing all of the hardships leading up to this moment, and the problems with the deal.

Still, I knew that I would treasure this moment for the rest of my life.

I pressed the button. Yes to Brexit. Yes to freedom. Yes to democracy. Yes.

Nigel leaves the Parliament to the world's media for the last time, never to return

Postscript

"That's it. It's over, done" – *Nigel Farage, after his final speech before leaving the European Parliament for the final time.*

The vote was passed by a huge margin: 621 votes in favour, 49 against and just 13 abstentions - it was never in doubt.

We enjoyed a final dinner together as MEPs that evening. It was a night that didn't seem to end. We were jubilant, ecstatic that our efforts had not been in vain. Perfect it may not have been, but the alternative would have been much worse.

Normality, or at least some semblance of normality, was something many of us looked forward to after seven months of madness, political wrangling, election after election, thousands of miles travelled, hundreds of speeches delivered and a final farewell. Not too shabby for a Party that didn't exist a year prior

Brexit Party MEPs lead the 'Brexodus Express' as they leave Brussels for the final time

to that momentous day. Little did we know at the time that normality would not be returning any time soon, that a virus as-yet-almost-unknown was multiplying at the other side of the world, soon to overshadow Brexit in many people's minds.

On the final day, a number of my colleagues walked out of the Parliament brandishing the "Brexodus Express", led by a Scottish bagpiper. Ann Widdecombe delivered a final goodbye, in the glare of what seemed like the entire world's press and broadcast media - before sharing a taxi with Jonathan Bullock on the way to the Gare du Midi for one final return journey home. The Brexit Party had made its mark in just seven months in the European Parliament, flanked by an incredibly talented team of MEPs who worked well together and stood up for democracy. The Brexit Party had reset Brexit, pulled it from the brink of disaster and forced our Government to make commitments.

As the clock struck midnight in London, huge crowds of supporters celebrated the biggest event in British history since victory in 1945. I am sad to say that I wasn't in London that evening: I was physically, emotionally and mentally drained from what was the most frustrating, exciting and significant year in British politics – not just my own lifetime. My emotions were very fragile in the weeks that passed: the many friendships and adversaries borne out of this decade of my life were no longer going to be a part of my day-to-day work. It was a strange feeling, but there was a deeper knowledge that it hadn't been a waste of time. We had been successful in winning the argument, and it was a year that I'll always look back on with fondness.

Yes, we had wanted the Government to take a strong negotiating stance, to try to win back our fishing waters, our laws and the ability to trade freely without being shackled to EU regulations. The Political Declaration was a major sticking point for many of us: there were too many commitments to the EU budget, EU defence force and keeping Northern Ireland in the EU customs union. These made us uneasy as to whether we would truly be free of the EU by the end of the transition period. But the Political Declaration did not have the same force as the Withdrawal Agreement. Many of the commitments only required the UK to 'consider' co-operation on these matters. Ben Habib put it brilliantly: that a repudiation of the political declaration is what would be needed to ensure that we no longer made commitments to the European Investment Bank and the EU defence force. We should remove ourselves cleanly to protect our internal market.

That is why the Brexit Party came into existence. That is why the Brexit Party continued to fight for a Brexit that delivered on the referendum result in 2016. With hindsight, perhaps we had underestimated the success of the Tory slogan of 'Get Brexit Done' during the General Election. It was a masterpiece of spin rather than substance.

There was undoubtedly a level of public Brexit fatigue, which the Conservatives capitalised upon without much real debate on the content of the new Withdrawal Agreement. It is very difficult to take on the machinery of such a well-polished communications strategy that the Tories had put together. Our experience of the Peterborough by-election had been an early taste of that. We had pushed the government as hard as we possibly could, and we had succeeded in forcing a number of concessions – not least of which was the commitment from Boris at the start of the General Election that he would not seek an extension to the transition period. We would not have stepped aside 317 of our candidates otherwise – a controversial decision, certainly, but one which was not taken lightly and still divides some of the former MEPs as well as supporters to this day.

Sometimes you have to balance what is at stake. At that time, with emotions running high, there was a genuine risk of a hung Parliament that could force a second referendum. A gambler in Vegas can lose an entire fortune in just three words: 'Let it ride'. As a keen poker player myself, I know that there's a time to take my chips from the table and cash out my winnings.

Perhaps continuing regardless and fighting all seats might have risked Brexit itself. Certainly not the outcome the Party that had fought for Brexit would have wanted! Others argue it may have given us some seats in Parliament to hold the Government to account during transition. These are all valid views, and ultimately there is no right answer. We all, in one way or another, chose to put country before party.

One thing is for sure:

Without the Brexit Party there would be no new Prime Minister. There would have been no revised treaty. There would have been no General Election mandate. We would have signed up to far worse than this deal under Theresa May.

There will, no doubt, be attempts to airbrush out our part in the year that changed politics. The establishment parties will claim Brexit as their victory. It's what they do: take credit for the work of others.

In fact, 2019 would never have been the year that changed politics without the Brexit Party, without our resounding victory in the European Elections, without forcing an untrustworthy Prime Minister out of office, without almost winning a Parliamentary seat just months after coming into existence, or without a proxy Leave alliance in the General Election.

Make no mistake, the Tory party had to change or face electoral oblivion. At least in Johnson, they do have someone who campaigned for a Leave vote rather than the Remain convictions of Theresa May.

I enjoyed working alongside my colleagues in Brussels and Strasbourg. I will never forget the passion of June Mummery and her drive for UK fishing rights, the knowledge and experience of Henrik Overgaard-Nielsen, or the support of Claire Fox and her brilliant speeches in the chamber. The excellent and supportive team of researchers and advisors should also get an important mention, many of whom I'd worked with many years previously. They'll be missed. The camaraderie of our team with a wide mix of political experience, ages and backgrounds has definitely made us friends for life. I doubt any future political organisation will ever recreate the togetherness we displayed, and it is that uniqueness - being such a melting pot of different people – which is what made the Brexit Party successful. That's what Nigel and Richard wanted to build all along, and it's what made us all stick together and support each other.

We had rebooted Brexit, stopped the gravy train and put country before party.

I hope that history will remember the Brexit Party as the catalyst that helped to make sure Brexit was 'done' and not ignore the 17.4 million people that asked our Government to take Britain out of the EU. That is our legacy. That is the legacy of not just the victory in the European Elections but the legacy of the many hundreds of thousands of people who helped deliver Brexit for over a quarter of a century, the legacy that stopped the Remain brigade from reversing democracy.

I've written this book not only as a memoir, not just because I hope you'll find it interesting to know what happened behind the scenes, but also to put on record what we did – and what we achieved.

I recall David Cameron's words as Prime Minister in 2013:

"I say to the British people: this will be your decision. And when that choice comes, you will have an important choice to make about our country's destiny."

It was our decision. We made that decision together, as a nation. The Brexit Party's legacy was to force that promise to be kept.. We shaped our country's destiny.

Let the record reflect what the Brexit Party achieved: Brexit.